NEW VANGUARD 266

FRENCH BATTLESHIPS 1914–45

RYAN K. NOPPEN   ILLUSTRATED BY PAUL WRIGHT

OSPREY PUBLISHING

Bloomsbury Publishing Plc

PO Box 883, Oxford, OX1 9PL, UK

1385 Broadway, 5th Floor, New York, NY 10018, USA

E-mail: info@ospreypublishing.com

www.ospreypublishing.com

OSPREY is a trademark of Osprey Publishing Ltd

First published in Great Britain in 2019

A catalogue record for this book is available from the British Library.

ISBN: PB 9781472818195; eBook 9781472818218;

ePDF 9781472818201; XML 9781472827500

19 20 21 22 23   10 9 8 7 6 5 4 3 2 1

Index by Fionbar Lyons
Typeset by PDQ Digital Media Solutions, Bungay, UK
Printed in China through World Print Ltd.

Artist's note

Readers may care to note that the original paintings from which the colour plates in this book were prepared are available for private sale. All reproduction copyright whatsoever is retained by the Publishers. All enquiries should be addressed to: p.wright1@btinternet.com
The Publishers regret that they can enter into no correspondence upon this matter.

Osprey Publishing supports the Woodland Trust, the UK's leading woodland conservation charity.

To find out more about our authors and books visit
www.ospreypublishing.com. Here you will find extracts, author interviews, details of forthcoming events and the option to sign up for our newsletter.

ACKNOWLEDGMENTS

The author wishes to thank his lovely wife Sarah, for putting up with another several months of chatter about old warships, and her French *bonne-maman*, who wonders who would read about such a subject.

GLOSSARY

Amiral – Admiral

Comité français de Libération nationale – French Committee of National Liberation, formed on 3 June 1943

Commandant en chef de la flotte méditerranéenne – Commander-in-Chief of the Mediterranean Fleet

Conseil de défense de l'Empire – General Charles de Gaulle's Free French government-in-exile

Conseil supérieur de la marine – Navy advisory board

Croiseur de Bataille – battlecruiser

Division des Écoles – Training Division

Division Navale de la Manche et de la mer du Nord – Naval Division of the Channel and the North Sea

Dreadnought – revolutionary battleship commissioned into the Royal Navy on 11 December 1906

en gardiennage d'Armistice – under the guard of the Armistice

escadre – squadron

Force de Raid – a squadron of fast warships initially based at Brest, 1939–40

Forces de Haute Mer – High Seas Forces, the main operational force of the Vichy fleet

Jeune École – new generation of officers, 1871–1900

Kaiserliche Marine – Imperial German Navy

Kleinkrieg – small war

kaiserliche und königliche (k.u.k.) Kriegsmarine – Austro-Hungarian Navy

Marine nationale française – French Navy

Mittelmeerdivision – German World War I Mediterranean Division

Parlement français – French parliament

programme naval de 1900 – a fleet law which authorized the construction of six new battleships

Regia Marina – Italian Royal Navy

Service technique des constructions navales – French navy's construction and technical department

1912 Statut Naval – passed on 30 March 1912, a fixed naval law which could not be radically altered by regime change

Vice-amiral – Vice admiral

CONTENTS

FRENCH BATTLESHIPS 1914–45

INTRODUCTION

In spite of its early technological and military achievement with the *Gloire* of 1859 – the world's first ocean-going ironclad warship – France's development of battleships for much of the Age of Steam was largely a tortured affair. Following the seeming inactivity of the French navy during the disastrous Franco-Prussian War, naval might became a significantly lesser national priority than rebuilding and strengthening France's army; a hard realization for a navy that traditionally had been second in strength only to Great Britain. For much of the period from 1871 to 1900, the navy fell under the influence of a new generation of officers, the *Jeune École*. As Great Britain was still France's foremost enemy, the Jeune École pushed for a new naval strategy of commerce raiding with fast cruisers (a strategy that had been recently well-utilized by Confederate commerce raiders in the American Civil War) and coastal defence by means of numerous squadrons of torpedo boats, using the recently developed technology of the self-propelled torpedo. The lower cost of the Jeune École's strategy appealed to French politicians, particularly socialist ones who wished to eclipse the power of the traditionalist 'aristocratic' officer corps of the navy. As traditionalists within French naval circles tended to promote the construction of battleships for a balanced battlefleet, battleship design and construction quickly ran afoul of partisan politics. From 1871 on, new capital ships were built individually and not immediately as a class. In theory this reactionary policy allowed for rigorous trials of the 'prototype' vessel and allowed for changes and improvements or, if need be, cancellation of the project before committing to construction of a complete class. In practice this resulted in a number of 'custom' battleships built in the 1880s and 1890s, which varied in terms of armament and machinery, a logistical mess. Politics, the Jeune École, construction irregularities and a lack of a uniform naval strategy due to 24 different naval ministries from 1880 to 1902 left the *Marine nationale française* (French Navy) with few effective battleships towards the end of the nineteenth century – at a time when a new naval power began to assert its presence across the waters of the world.

The German *Flottengesetze*, or Fleet Laws, of the late nineteenth and early twentieth centuries facilitated the creation of a powerful German blue-water navy, the goal of which was to challenge the long-held worldwide supremacy of the British Royal Navy. Another consequence of this naval

Image from the period publication *Le Petit Journal* detailing naval exercises of the *Marine nationale française* in 1908. The image of the small submarine set against an older capital ship appropriately summed up the composition of the French fleet at the turn of the century. Obsolete capital ships of varying designs and large numbers of experimental submarines and torpedo boats represented the late 19th-century conflict between advocates of a battlefleet and proponents of the *Jeune École*. (Photo by Ann Ronan Pictures/ Print Collector/Getty Images)

commitment was the rapid displacement of the Marine Nationale as the world's second most powerful navy by the upstart German *Kaiserliche Marine* (Imperial German Navy). At the turn of the century France's only ally was Russia; theoretically the Marine Nationale had to plan for war scenarios against its traditional rival, Great Britain, the powers of the Triple Alliance (Germany, Austria-Hungary and Italy), or a combination of any of the said powers – all at a time when the operational and construction strategies of the Marine Nationale were in a relatively confused state. In 1899 Jean de Lanessan, Minister of Marine under the moderate government of Prime Minister Pierre Waldeck-Rousseau, recognized the need for a consistent naval strategy, a balanced fleet and the need for homogenous classes of battleships. De Lanessan succeeded in securing the *programme naval de 1900*, a fleet law which authorized the construction of six new

battleships (the Patrie class) which were on a par with foreign contemporaries, all to be laid down before the beginning of 1907. De Lanessan's plan envisioned a fleet centred around 28 battleships and assumed that subsequent classes of new battleships would follow the lead he established. The assumption of power of a radical leftist regime under Prime Minister Émile Combes in 1902 disrupted the balance carefully established over the previous three years. The new Minister of Marine, Camille Pelletan, advocated for a return to the strategy of the Jeune École largely as a political manoeuvre to destabilize the power of the naval officer corps. Pelletan delayed the construction of the Patrie class battleships in order to subsidize experimental projects, particularly submarines, which rarely showed practical combat application. By the time Pelletan left office in January 1905, not one of the Patrie class battleships had been completed; nor were any complete when the revolutionary *Dreadnought* was commissioned into the Royal Navy on 11 December 1906.

Danton class semi-dreadnought *Diderot* being launched at the yards of Ateliers et Chantiers de Penhoët in St Nazaire on 20 April 1909. (Photo by De Agostini/Biblioteca Ambrosiana/Getty Images)

SEMI-DREADNOUGHTS AND DREADNOUGHTS OF THE MARINE NATIONALE

Danton class

The tenure of the more moderate Gaston Thomson as Minister of Marine, which began in January 1905, allowed the Marine Nationale to return to the parameters of the programme naval de 1900 and resume the expansion of its battlefleet. The immediate priority was to see to the completion of the Patrie class pre-dreadnought battleships. Thanks to Pelletan's meddling, the Patrie class vessels entered service between January 1907 and September 1908; construction times ranged from five to six years, compared to the average build time of three years for the five Deutschland class battleships laid down in Germany from 1903 to 1905. Both Thomson and the *Conseil supérieur de la marine* (navy advisory board) in the summer of 1905 advocated for a larger new class of battleship with an overall heavier armament than the Patries. The primary armament was to be four of the new Canon de 305mm/45 modèle 1906 guns and the intermediate armament was to be made up of 240mm guns, compared to the 194mm guns in the Patrie class vessels. Design work began in the summer of 1905 and it was hoped to lay down the new vessels in the following year. Despite knowledge of the all-big-gun *Dreadnought* being built, the Marine Nationale felt confident in its new battleship design as the British were simultaneously building the two vessels of the Lord Nelson class both armed with primary and intermediate batteries; furthermore, the Japanese laid down the semi-dreadnoughts of the Satsuma class in 1905 and Austro-Hungarian shipyards laid down

Semi-dreadnought *Voltaire*.
(Author's collection)

the semi-dreadnoughts of the Radetzky class as late as 1907. At the time the new French design was more powerful than all other pre-dreadnought battleships coming into service abroad. The results of the recent Battle of Tsushima, fought on 27–28 May 1905, also appeared to validate the Marine Nationale's decision to retain a powerful intermediate battery in its new battleship design; much of the damage inflicted upon the Russians at Tsushima came at medium-range distances from Japanese intermediate batteries, which had a higher rate of fire than the primary batteries aboard their battleships.

The decision upon a final design was delayed into 1907 however, due to debates about armament arrangements and method of propulsion (vertical triple-expansion engines versus new turbines), but by that time the *Parlement français* (French parliament) had approved funding for six new battleships; this government decision was less generous than it was practical. The timelines of prior and current capital ship construction tended to be exceptionally slow, let alone arbitrary, and with the naval arms race between Great Britain and Germany increasing in tempo, anything which could assist in increasing the pace of French battleship construction was deemed valuable. The battleships of the new Danton class were completed as follows: *Voltaire* at Forges et Chantiers de la Méditerranée in La Seyne-sur-Mer (laid down 8 June 1907, launched 16 January 1909, commissioned 5 August 1911); *Condorcet* at Ateliers et Chantiers de la Loire in Saint-Nazaire (laid down 23 August 1907, launched 19 April 1909, commissioned 25 July 1911); *Diderot* at Ateliers et Chantiers de Penhoët in Saint-Nazaire (laid down 23 August 1907, launched 20 April 1909, commissioned 25 July 1911); *Danton* at Arsenal de Brest (laid down 9 January 1908, launched 4 July 1909, commissioned 24 July 1911); *Mirabeau* at Arsenal de Lorient (laid down 4 May 1908, launched 28 October 1909, commissioned 1 August 1911); *Vergniaud* at Forges et Chantiers de la Gironde near Bordeaux (laid down July 1908, launched 12 April 1910, commissioned 18 December 1911). (See Plate A for additional details about the Danton class.)

Vice-Amiral Augustin Boué de Lapeyrère, the visionary yet practical French minister of marine who secured the construction of France's first class of dreadnought battleships and commander of the 1re Armée Navale for the first year of World War I. (Library of Congress LC-B2-3252-12)

Danton class specifications

Dimensions	length: 146.6m; beam: 25.8m; draught: 8.44m
Full Displacement	19,763 tons
Ship's Complement	856 men
Armament	four Canon de 305mm/45 Modèle 1906 guns in two twin turrets (305mm/45 gun had a range at 12 degrees elevation of 14,500m, could penetrate 279mm of armour at 10,000m with a 435.5kg armour-piercing shell, and had an elevation range of -5 to 12 degrees; 85 rounds were carried per gun and 1–2 rounds could be fired per minute); 12 Canon de 240mm/50 Modèle 1902–1906 intermediate guns in six twin turrets (240mm/50 gun had a range at 45 degrees elevation of 23,812m, could penetrate 206mm of armour at 10,000m with a 220kg armour-piercing shell, and had an elevation range of -5 to 45 degrees; 100 rounds were carried per gun and three rounds could be fired per minute); 16 Canon de 75mm/62.5 Modèle 1908 Schneider quick-fire guns mounted in open, unarmoured gun ports; eight Canon Hotchkiss à tir rapide de 47mm modèle 1902 quick-fire guns, four mounted around each mast; two submerged 450mm torpedo tubes
Machinery	four Parsons direct-drive turbines, coal-fired by 26 Niclausse (*Condorcet*, *Diderot* and *Vergniaud*) or Belleville (*Danton*, *Mirabeau* and *Voltaire*) boilers, producing up to 22,500 indicated horsepower and driving four screws up to a maximum speed of 19.25 knots
Maximum Range	3,500 nautical miles at 10 knots
Protection	armoured belt: 250mm at the centre tapering to 180mm at the ends; conning tower: 266mm; barbettes: 246mm; primary turrets: 340mm on front, 260mm on the sides and rear, and 72mm on the top; intermediate turrets: 225mm on front, 188mm on the sides and rear, and 51mm on the top; armoured deck: 48mm

Courbet class

Vice-Amiral Augustin Boué de Lapeyrère brought a better degree of clarity with regard to fleet planning than his recent predecessors had when he became Minister of Marine in July 1909. It was clear to the veteran naval officer that France's economy as well as its industrial and naval infrastructure could not realistically complete the 45-battleship fleet plan recommended by the Conseil supérieur de la marine the year before. Lapeyrère admitted

DANTON CLASS SEMI-DREADNOUGHT

The Danton class semi-dreadnoughts were something of an outdated-yet-modern anomaly at a time when Great Britain was simultaneously laying down the six vessels of its Bellerophon and St Vincent classes of dreadnoughts and Germany the four vessels of its Nassau class. The Dantons were even an anomaly among the handful of other semi-dreadnought designs under construction in Great Britain, Japan and Austria-Hungary. Whereas the primary and intermediate turrets of the Lord Nelson, Satsuma and Radetzky class vessels possessed a more modern, angular design with a lower silhouette, the Dantons retained the older, pronounced cylindrical turrets of previous French battleship designs – an almost-19th-century look, particularly with the retention of the traditional French tumblehome hull. The *Marine Nationale*'s continued belief that engagements would take place at intermediate ranges affected the capabilities of the guns in the primary turrets in that their maximum elevation was only 12 degrees; it was surprised to learn after World War I that the primary guns aboard the semi-dreadnoughts of the Radetzky class were originally designed to have a maximum elevation of 20 degrees, the Austro-Hungarian *k.u.k. Kriegsmarine* (Austro-Hungarian Imperial and Royal Navy) anticipating future engagements at longer ranges (the British would increase the maximum elevation for the primary guns of the Lord Nelson class from 13.5 degrees to 16 degrees during World War I). Another key distinction between the Dantons and their foreign semi-dreadnought contemporaries was the use of turbine propulsion. *Dreadnought* was the first battleship to be powered by turbines and the Dantons were the third class of battleship in the world, and first non-British, to be likewise equipped. A final distinction between the Dantons and foreign semi-dreadnoughts was that classes built abroad only consisted of two to three vessels; the six Dantons and their delayed construction times committed the Marine Nationale to more ships of an obsolescent type and consumed considerably more construction effort, which ultimately would have been better spent on dreadnought construction.

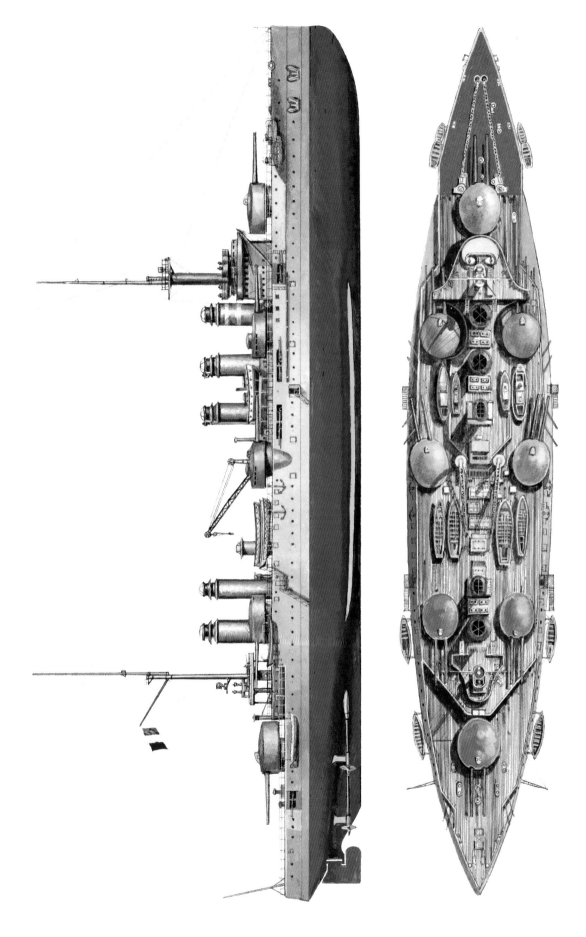

Courbet class dreadnought
Jean Bart in the final stages of
construction in the Arsenal de
Brest. (Author's collection)

that naval parity with the rapidly growing Kaiserliche Marine could not be achieved and was willing to run the risk of depending upon a benevolent Royal Navy to contain any seaborne threats from Germany via the North Sea and Atlantic in the event of war; the Entente Cordiale signed between France and Great Britain in April 1904, while not a formal alliance, did make it clear that both powers recognized the growing naval threat from Germany. He argued that the primary strategic focus for the Marine Nationale should be dominance of the Mediterranean and that new naval construction allotments should be geared to countering the *k.u.k. Kriegsmarine* (Austro-Hungarian Navy) and the Italian *Regia Marina* (Italian Royal Navy). After a year of research Lapeyrère proposed to the Parlement a revised building plan, to be completed by 1920, of 28 battleships (counting the vessels of the Patrie pre-dreadnought and Danton semi-dreadnought classes), ten cruisers, 52 destroyers, 94 submarines and 10 colonial vessels. With regard to battleship construction the Minister of Marine proposed the following schedule of new vessels laid down by year: 2 (1910), 2 (1911), 3 (1912), 2 (1913), 2 (1914), 4 (1915), 0 (1916) and 2 (1917). Lapeyrère was able to convince the Parlement to approve the first stage of his building plan and funding was provided in the 1910 national budget for two new battleships; two more battleships would be authorized the following year as well. The design selected for construction in 1910 had its origins in a design study authorized by Gaston Thomson two years earlier. Toward the end of 1907, at the urging of Thomson, the *Service technique des constructions navales* (French navy's construction and technical department) prepared a design for a larger semi-dreadnought, essentially an improved Danton class unit, as well as a new dreadnought design which dispensed with the intermediate batteries and mounted twelve 305mm primary guns; triple and quadruple primary turret configurations were also examined, but were considered too experimental at the time. In December 1908 the Conseil supérieur de la marine decided to pursue a dreadnought design, but vacillated on the armament layout and protection arrangements.

After taking office Lapeyrère outlined the parameters for a dreadnought which could be built without undue delay in French shipyards and pushed the Service technique des constructions navales to rapidly finalize a design; the Marine Nationale was already well behind in the development of dreadnoughts compared to the Royal Navy and the Kaiserliche Marine, but it was also falling behind its Mediterranean rivals. In April 1909 a security breach revealed to the public the k.u.k. Kriegsmarine's plan for a new class of four dreadnoughts, which in turn prompted the Regia Marina to lay down its first dreadnought that June, ultimately kicking off a new naval arms

Parsons direct-drive turbines to be installed in *Jean Bart*. Despite France's tardy reluctance to abandon multiple heavy gun calibres on its battleships, the Marine Nationale was the second naval power in the world to adopt turbine propulsion for its capital ships, starting with the Danton class semi-dreadnoughts. (Author's collection)

race among the Mediterranean powers. The final design for the Courbet class dreadnoughts was finalized in the first half of 1910 and orders for the first two vessels were placed on 11 August, while the remaining two were ordered a year later. The four dreadnoughts of the Courbet class were completed as follows: *Courbet* at Arsenal de Lorient (laid down 1 September 1910, launched 23 September 1911, commissioned 19 November 1913); *Jean Bart* at Arsenal de Brest (laid down 15 November 1910, launched 22 September 1911, commissioned 19 November 1913); *Paris* at Forges et Chantiers de la Méditerranée (laid down 10 November 1911, launched 28 September 1912, commissioned 1 August 1914); *France* at Ateliers et Chantiers de la Loire (laid down 30 November 1911, launched 7 November 1912, commissioned 10 October 1914). (See Plate B for additional details about the Courbet class.)

Courbet class specifications

Dimensions	length: 166m, beam: 27m, draught: 9.04m
Full Displacement	25,579 tons
Ship's Complement	1,115 men
Armament	12 Canon de 305mm/45 Modèle 1910 guns in six twin turrets (similar characteristics to the 305mm/45 Modèle1906 guns of the Danton class); 22 Canon de 138.6mm/55 Modèle 1910 secondary guns located in single casemate mounts (138.6mm/55 gun had a range at 25 degrees elevation of 15,100m with a 31.5kg high-explosive shell and had an elevation range of -7 to 25 degrees; 275 rounds were carried per gun and five to six rounds could be fired per minute); four Canon Hotchkiss à tir rapide de 47mm modèle 1902 quick-fire guns mounted fore around the conning tower; four submerged 450mm torpedo tubes
Machinery	four Parsons direct-drive turbines, coal-fired by 24 Niclausse (*Courbet*) or Belleville (*France*, *Jean Bart* and *Paris*) boilers, producing up to 28,000 indicated horsepower and driving four screws up to a maximum speed of 21 knots
Maximum Range	4,200 nautical miles at 10 knots
Protection	armoured belt: 270mm at the centre tapering to 180mm at the ends; casemates: 180mm; conning tower: 300mm; barbettes: 280mm; turrets: 290mm on front, 400mm on the rear, 290mm on the sides and 72mm on the top; armoured deck: 48mm amidships tapering to 30mm on the ends

Jean Bart photographed during World War I. (Author's collection)

Bretagne class

Amiral Lapeyrère left the Ministry of Marine in March 1911 but his successor, Théophile Delcassé, shared the admiral's pragmatic assessment of France's naval capabilities as well as his vision of a powerful Mediterranean battle fleet. After much debate, the Parlement approved Lapeyrère's building plan as the 1912 *Statut Naval*, passed on 30 March 1912, a fixed naval law which could not be radically altered by regime change and thus allowed for

B

COURBET CLASS DREADNOUGHT

At first glance the ships of the Courbet class represented a modern step forward in French naval construction. The ships overall had lower silhouettes compared to the Dantons, their primary batteries were housed in modern-shaped turrets and the hull had vertical sides (in order to accommodate the wing primary turrets) as opposed to the tumblehome hulls of the Dantons. With the Courbets the Marine Nationale finally accepted the international standard of the dreadnought battleship, but despite being laid down in 1910–11 they clearly represented the first generation of dreadnought design. The wing turrets amidships had become an outdated arrangement as other navies were adopting the all-centreline location for their primary turrets aboard their dreadnoughts, as pioneered by the United States Navy. The dimensions of the largest graving docks in French shipyards limited the size of new battleship construction, particularly length (the Courbets were only 19.4m longer than the Dantons), which forced the maximum utilization of available space. Austro-Hungarian shipyards possessed similar limitations but the k.u.k. Kriegsmarine's Tegetthoff class dreadnoughts, the first laid down in July 1910, were 14m shorter than the Courbets, and they had a more powerful broadside – the Tegetthoffs had all of their primary batteries located along the centreline and each utilized four triple turrets; the Regia Marina's *Dante Alighieri* likewise had four triple turrets along the centreline. While the *Service technique des constructions navales* was researching triple and quadruple turret arrangements, Lapeyrère felt that the time required for their development would unnecessarily hold back the Marine Nationale's dreadnought building programme in relation to its Mediterranean rivals. Another anachronistic feature of the Courbets' primary armament arrangement was that the turrets retained the maximum gun elevation of only 12 degrees, which the Dantons had. French naval strategists still refused to believe that effective long-range gunnery battles could not be fought, owing to the limitations of the fire control equipment of the time. Despite these shortcomings, the Courbets compared similarly to the Italian and Austro-Hungarian first classes of dreadnoughts in terms of speed and protection. Shown here is *Courbet* in her 1914 configuration.

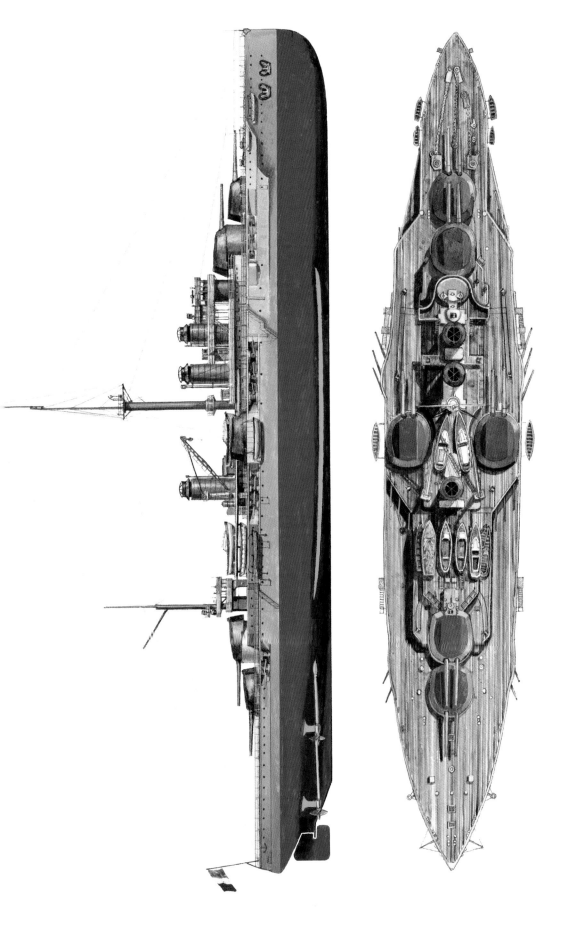

a measure of dedicated strategic planning. According to the construction timetable advocated by Lapeyrère, the 1912 Statut Naval allowed spending for three new dreadnoughts in 1912 and the Marine Nationale wasted no time in submitting orders for them. The size of French graving docks had remained the same since the laying down of the Courbet class, so the Conseil supérieur de la marine advised the Service technique des constructions navales to utilize dimensions similar to the Courbet class in the new design. Work had begun on new, significantly larger graving docks at Brest and Toulon in 1909, but their completion was not anticipated until 1915. This decision was also due to the need to match new construction in Italy and Austria-Hungary. During the summer of 1910 the Regia Marina had laid down the three vessels of its Conte di Cavour class of dreadnoughts and had already followed them with the two ships of the Andrea Doria class in early 1912; the k.u.k. Kriegsmarine, meanwhile, had laid down two additional Tegetthoff class dreadnoughts in January 1912, giving the powers of the Triple Alliance ten dreadnoughts under construction compared to only four in France by the beginning of April 1912. There was no time to wait for infrastructure improvements to allow for larger vessels if the Marine Nationale was to keep pace with its Mediterranean rivals, let alone maintain the building schedule of the 1912 Statut Naval. The new Bretagne class of dreadnoughts was very similar to the Courbets, having almost exactly the same protection arrangement, the same type and number of secondary guns (although grouped in a different casemate arrangement) and a slightly modified propulsion arrangement which produced the same horsepower and maximum speed.

The main distinction between the two classes was heavier primary armament in the Bretagnes. In 1909 the Royal Navy had selected 13.5in (343mm) guns to arm its dreadnoughts and battlecruisers, beginning with the Orion class, and by the beginning of 1912 it was testing new 15in (381mm) guns to arm the vessels of its Queen Elizabeth class. As 350mm and 381mm guns were likewise under development by other major naval powers which had embraced the concept of the super-dreadnought, the Conseil supérieur de la marine mandated the use of the newly developed 340mm/45 gun. The heavier weight of the guns and their larger turrets meant that only five twin primary turrets could be accommodated in the restricted hull, but they were all located along the centreline, allowing the Bretagne class vessels

Bretagne class dreadnought *Provence* in 1915. (Author's collection)

to fire all of their primary batteries in a broadside. While the new 340mm gun was smaller than those being used or developed abroad, it was judged by the Service technique des constructions navales to be the heaviest calibre weapon in domestic production that could effectively equip a dreadnought built to the maximum dimensions allowed in French graving docks. Ironically the 340mm turrets were still limited to a maximum elevation of only 12 degrees, resulting in a maximum range of only 14,500m; whereas the 305mm guns of the Italian dreadnoughts under construction had a maximum range of 24,000m at a maximum turret elevation of 20 degrees. The decision of the Conseil supérieur de la marine to maintain a fixed construction schedule in an attempt to match construction in Italy and Austria-Hungary prohibited the Marine Nationale from developing a class of true super-dreadnoughts before World War I, but fortunately the conflict began before either the Regia Marina or the k.u.k. Kriegsmarine were able to lay down their planned classes of super-dreadnoughts. The three dreadnoughts of the Bretagne class were completed as follows: *Bretagne* at Arsenal de Brest (laid down 22 July 1912, launched 21 April 1913, commissioned 10 February 1916); *Provence* at Arsenal de Lorient (laid down 21 April 1912, launched 20 April 1913, commissioned 1 March 1916); *Lorraine* at Ateliers et Chantiers de Penhoët (laid down 7 November 1912, launched 30 September 1913, commissioned 10 March 1916).

Aft primary turrets of *Bretagne*. The 340mm guns of the Bretagne class were the most powerful to be mounted on a French capital ship before World War II. (Naval History and Heritage Command NH 42845)

Bretagne class specifications

Dimensions	length: 166m; beam: 27m; draught: 9.1m
Full Displacement	26,600 tons
Ship's Complement	1,193 men
Armament	ten Canon de 340mm/45 Modèle 1912 guns in five twin turrets (340mm/45 gun had a range at 12 degrees elevation of 14,500m and had an elevation range of -5 to 12 degrees; 100 rounds were carried per gun and two rounds could be fired per minute); twenty-two Canon de 138.6mm/55 Modèle 1910 secondary guns located in single casemate mounts; two Canon Hotchkiss à tir rapide de 47mm modèle 1902 quick-fire guns mounted fore around the conning tower; four submerged 450mm torpedo tubes
Machinery	four Parsons direct-drive turbines, coal-fired by 24 Niclausse (*Bretagne*), 24 Belleville (*Lorraine*) or 18 Guyot du Temple (*Provence*) boilers, producing up to 28,000 indicated horsepower and driving four screws up to a maximum speed of 21 knots
Maximum Range	4,700 nautical miles at 10 knots
Protection	armoured belt: 250mm at the centre tapering to 180mm at the ends; casemates: 160mm; conning tower: 300mm; barbettes: 280mm; turrets: 340mm on front, 400mm on the rear, 340mm on the sides and 72mm on the top; armoured deck: 48mm amidships tapering to 30mm on the ends.

FRENCH BATTLESHIP OPERATIONS 1914–1919

The lack of an enemy battlefleet

Owing to pre-war contingency planning – possibly having to face the combined naval forces of Germany, Austria-Hungary and Italy in the Mediterranean upon the outbreak of a general war – the Marine Nationale had concentrated its most powerful and capable units at Toulon and Bizerte in the western Mediterranean. Vice-Amiral Lapeyrère, now *commandant en chef de la flotte méditerranéenne* (Commander-in-Chief of the Mediterranean Fleet), commanded the *1re Armée Navale* which was composed of the two operational Courbet class dreadnoughts, all of the Danton class semi-dreadnoughts, eight pre-dreadnoughts and accompanying armoured cruisers, destroyers and torpedo boats. In the early morning hours of 3 August 1914 Lapeyrère and the 1re Armée Navale put to sea and headed for French North Africa, intent on convoying troop ships carrying the XIX Corps from Algeria to metropolitan France, a critical part of the French High Command's pre-war mobilization plan. After the French declaration of war on Germany the following morning, Lapeyrère was ordered to take offensive action against the German *Mittelmeerdivision* (Mediterranean Division), composed of the battlecruiser *Goeben* and the light cruiser *Breslau*. That morning the German warships briefly appeared off the Algerian ports of Bône and Philippeville, bombarded them and then retired eastward, having received instructions from Berlin to proceed to Constantinople – a course unknown to both the Marine Nationale and the Royal Navy, as both assumed that the German vessels would sail westward and make a break for the Atlantic. When Lapeyrère learned of the bombardments he chose not to pursue *Goeben* and *Breslau* as his battleships (or even his armoured cruisers) did not have the speed necessary to overtake them; furthermore, he was aware that the Germans were fitting out a number of ocean liners as auxiliary cruisers in the western Mediterranean, fast warships which could pose a threat to French seaborne troop movements. Instead he thought it wise to convoy the troop ships, which sailed according to a fixed mobilization schedule that the Ministry of War refused to alter. Lapeyrère was later criticized for not taking aggressive action against *Goeben* and *Breslau* despite the slower speeds of his battleships and the lack of intelligence of the Germans' course and destination. To the French and British leadership Lapeyrère was a convenient scapegoat for the Mittelmeersdivision's escape and subsequent role in bringing the Ottoman Empire into the war on the side of the Central Powers.

C

BRETAGNE CLASS DREADNOUGHT

The 1912 *Statut Naval* allowed for an impressive expansion of the French battlefleet and new and larger graving docks, that finally allowed for capital ships larger than the Courbet class, which were laid down on the eve of World War I. The conflict devastated France's economy however, leaving no funds for immediate post-war capital ship construction. The Washington Naval Treaty, signed by France in early 1922, also prohibited new capital ship construction among its signatories for ten years. The only way for the Marine Nationale to maintain a relatively modern battlefleet into the post-war years was to continually modernize its existing battleships, despite the fact that their firepower and protection were inferior to the latest classes of ships completed in Great Britain, the United States and Japan prior to 1922. *Courbet*, *Jean Bart* and *Paris* underwent two modernization periods in the early 1920s and early 1930s in which they received large tripod foremasts, improved fire control equipment and had their primary turrets altered to allow their guns to be raised to a maximum of 23 degrees, increasing the maximum range of the 305mm guns to 26,000m. The three vessels of the Bretagne class likewise had the maximum gun elevation allowed by their primary turrets increased to 23 degrees and were equipped with modern fire control equipment. Being newer units however, more was invested in the refurbishment of their machinery and they had new oil-fired boilers installed. In 1934–35 *Lorraine* had her amidships primary turret removed and replaced with a hangar which could accommodate three aircraft and a catapult mounted above. On each side of the hangar four 100mm twin-mounted heavy anti-aircraft guns were installed. Shown here is *Lorraine* as she appeared when commissioned and also after her mid-1930s modernization.

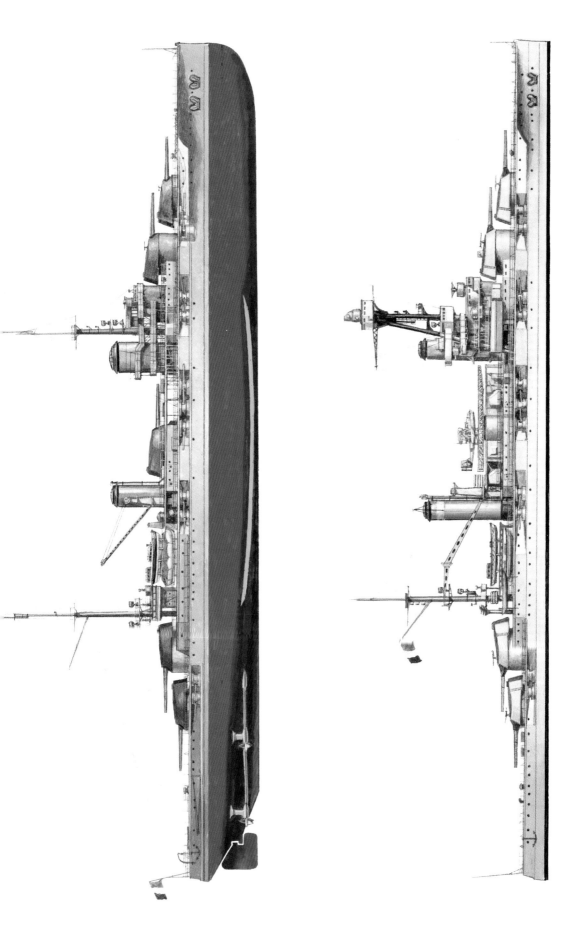

France (left) at Toulon with the liners Savoie (centre) and Gallia (right). The battleships of the 1re Armée Navale were engaged in escorting troop convoys from Algeria to France when the Goeben and Breslau conducted their North African raid on 4 August 1914. (Author's collection)

Period postcard showing the sinking of the Austro-Hungarian protected cruiser Zenta off the Montenegrin coast on 16 August 1914 by the 1re Armée Navale. This obsolescent 2,503-ton cruiser was the largest warship engaged by French semi-dreadnoughts and dreadnoughts during World War I. (Author's collection)

Ironically, this occasion would prove to be the closest German and French capital ships would come to each other for the entire war.

After learning of the escape of *Goeben* and *Breslau* to the east and that they no longer posed a threat to the Algerian convoys, Lapeyrère left his older pre-dreadnoughts to remain on convoy duty while he sailed with the bulk of the 1re Armée Navale for Malta, arriving there on 13 August; Lapeyrère had been advised to prepare for naval operations against Austria-Hungary, upon whom France declared war on 12 August. Four days later Lapeyrère took the 1re Armée Navale into the Adriatic, intent on raising the Austro-Hungarian blockade of the Montenegrin coast and in the process luring the bulk of the k.u.k. Kriegsmarine into a decisive battle. While off Antivari, Lapeyrère's forces surprised and overwhelmed the old Austro-Hungarian protected cruiser *Zenta* with an unnecessarily heavy barrage. *Zenta* went down with her ensign still flying while her consort, the destroyer *Ulan*, evaded the French and escaped. The engagement of 16 August was, tangibly speaking, a hollow victory, especially as the k.u.k. Kriegsmarine's commander, Admiral Anton Haus, wisely refused to sortie his battlefleet into a battle which would be fought on the enemy's terms. It was soberly instructional, however, as Lapeyrère quickly realized the strategic limitations of his forces. The 1re Armée Navale had no modern and fast light cruisers and Lapeyrère's armoured cruisers lacked the speed necessary to pursue the light cruisers and destroyers of the k.u.k. Kriegsmarine (as evidenced by the escape of *Ulan*). The majority of its destroyers and torpedo boats were ill-suited for lengthy high seas operations and suffered from frequent mechanical problems; their operational ranges were also very limited. This meant that any operations against the primary k.u.k. Kriegsmarine base at Pola or elsewhere in the upper Adriatic could not be conducted by French light units.

Logistics ultimately proved the greatest challenge to Lapeyrère and his warships at the outset of the war, as Malta was the closest Allied base to the Adriatic theatre of operations and the Marine Nationale was not well equipped with supply vessels and colliers. Throughout the first year and a half of the war the units of the 1re Armée Navale coaled and resupplied, on a limited basis, throughout the bays and inlets of the Ionian Sea, due to the pro-Allied sympathies of Greek Prime Minister Eleftherios Venizelos. At the time it proved to be a complicated and inconvenient solution as King Constantine I of Greece and much of the Greek government and military leadership insisted upon Greek neutrality in the war and protested to Allied governments about their naval use of Greek coastal waters. Lapeyrère made several raids with the 1re Armée Navale along the Albanian and Dalmatian coasts throughout the remainder of 1914, but they proved to be

only pin-pricks against Austro-Hungarian coastal defences and Haus refused to sail the k.u.k. Kriegsmarine's battlefleet out of Pola. Unknown to the French, Haus was determined to fight a campaign of *Kleinkrieg* (small war) – consisting of hit-and-run raids against the Allies conducted with fast light cruisers, destroyers and torpedo boats, or attacks with U-boats – and preserve his battlefleet as a fleet-in-being. Lapeyrère witnessed Kleinkrieg at first hand on 21 December 1914, when *Jean Bart* was struck on her port bow by a torpedo fired from the Austro-Hungarian U-boat *U-12*. *Jean Bart* was able to limp back to Malta; Lapeyrère realized the danger posed to his battleships and withdrew them to the Ionian Sea and Malta, leaving his armoured cruisers to patrol the entrances to the Adriatic.

For the battleships of the 1re Armée Navale, 1915 proved to be a lethargic year. The constant state of semi-readiness to intercept a potential, yet never-coming, foray from the k.u.k. Kriegsmarine's battlefleet, combined with the inability to effectively curtail Haus' Kleinkrieg campaign, created a bitterly frustrating situation for Lapeyrère and his battleship crews. The sinking of the armoured cruiser *Léon Gambetta* by the Austro-Hungarian *U-5* on 27 August compelled Lapeyrère to only deploy light units on patrol duties. Like Haus, Lapeyrère was unwilling to lose any capital ships in a piece-meal fashion and was forced to keep his battlefleet intact – a fleet-in-being to counter another fleet-in-being. After Italy entered the war on 23 May 1915, Lapeyrère left the patrols of the entrance of the Adriatic to the Regia Marina and took his battleships back to Malta and Bizerte. Dispirited by the strategic situation faced by the 1re Armée Navale, Lapeyrère resigned on 10 October 1915 and was replaced by Vice-Amiral Louis-René Dartige du Fournet. The 1re Armée Navale's battleships saw no action or change of routine for the next six months. In April 1916, following the Malta Conference of 9 March 1916 between the Royal Navy, Marine Nationale and Regia Marina, Dartige du Fournet began basing the battleships of the 1re Armée Navale at Corfu and the harbour of Argostoli on the island of Cephalonia in the Ionian Sea. Despite the protests of the Greek government, the French occupied Corfu on 11 January 1916 to provide a base of operations for the Serbian Army-in-Exile as well as a safe haven for refugees from the Balkans.

Over the summer the new dreadnoughts *Bretagne*, *Lorraine* and *Provence* became operational and were assigned to the 1re Armée Navale. Anchorages on Corfu and at Argostoli finally gave the 1re Armée Navale a forward operating base close to the Adriatic, but chronic shortages of coal, which had to be delivered from other French bases, allowed for only minimal exercise cruises. With the exception of supporting Allied intervention

French lookouts scanning the surrounding seas aboard one of the Courbet class dreadnoughts with another sailing behind. German and Austro-Hungarian U-boats, instead of Austro-Hungarian and Italian battleships, became the primary menace to French capital ships throughout the Mediterranean – an ironic and successful application of *Jeune École* strategies by the Central Powers. (Photo by Hulton Archive/Getty Images)

Vessels of the 1re Armée Navale anchored at Corfu during World War I. One of the Bretagne class dreadnoughts is near the centre of the photograph. (Photo by adoc-photos/Corbis via Getty Images)

operations in Greece in late 1916 and early 1917, the battleships of the 1re Armée Navale largely remained inactive in their Ionian anchorages for the remainder of the war (see Plate D for details about French battleship operations during the Greek internal unrest in 1916). Only occasional trips for maintenance at Malta, Toulon or Bizerte offered a change of scenery, but these sailings were not without their dangers. On 19 March 1917, *Danton* was returning to Corfu from a refit at Toulon when she was struck by two torpedoes on her

Danton listing to port after being struck by two torpedoes from the German *U-64* on 19 March 1917. (Wikimedia Commons/anonymous/Gallica. fr/public domain)

starboard side fired from the German *U-64* south of Sardinia. At first it appeared that the flooding could be contained and her engines were still operational, but an unclosed watertight door allowed water into the portside passageways, quickly increasing the list to port; 23 minutes after being hit, *Danton* capsized and sank.

Frustration, mutiny and post-war limitations

The ongoing lack of coal, the constant threat of U-boat attack and the continuing inaction of the k.u.k. Kriegsmarine's battlefleet kept the 1re Armée Navale's dreadnoughts inactive for most of 1918. The threat of a new enemy fleet in the eastern Mediterranean, however, compelled the Marine Nationale to dispatch the semi-dreadnoughts *Condorcet*, *Diderot*, *Mirabeau* and *Vergniaud* to join a new Allied fleet forming in the Aegean in June 1918. The previous month the Germans had occupied the primary Russian Black Sea naval base at Sevastopol and had begun negotiations with the Bolshevik government for the surrender of all the vessels of the Black Sea Fleet. The

THE BATTLE OF ATHENS, 1 DECEMBER 1916

Although the battleships of the Marine Nationale would not experience battle with an enemy fleet during World War I, they would find themselves embroiled in two civil conflicts within the greater Mediterranean theatre. The first of these was in the period of Greek political upheaval referred to as the National Schism. In September 1915, the French landed the *Armée d'Orient* in the Greek port of Salonica, and the force was sent northwards to assist the hard-pressed Serbian army, facing a major Central Powers offensive. This constituted a violation of Greece's neutrality and began a period of civil unrest in Greece between the supporters of the pro-Allied prime minister Eleftherios Venizelos and the pro-Central Powers monarch King Constantine I. In the autumn of 1916 supporters of Venizelos created a separate government in Salonica that openly favoured the Allies and later declared war on the Central Powers. Following this coup the Allies, in particular the French, pressed the royal Greek government to demobilize its armed forces and consent to a more pro-Allied neutrality. On 10 October 1916 Amiral Dartige du Fournet, aboard *Provence*, sailed a force drawn from the *1re Armée Navale* into the Bay of Salamis and seized and disarmed the Greek fleet. In late November the French government demanded the arms and ammunition from the royal Greek government to arm pro-Allied Greek volunteers on the Salonica front. When the deadline for the handover passed Dartige du Fournet sailed into Pireaus harbour near Athens on 1 December and went ashore with a landing party, believing that this show of force would cause the Greeks to give in. As the admiral and his sailors and marines marched into Athens, the Greek military units stationed there refused to turn over any weapons and a battle broke out. The French were caught by surprise and for a time Dartige du Fournet was cut off from the harbour; the semi-dreadnought *Mirabeau* was briefly called upon for fire support. A ceasefire was eventually negotiated, but after realizing his forces were vastly outnumbered, Dartige du Fournet fell back on Pireaus and his vessels while the Greek royalists celebrated a victory. Eleven days later Dartige du Fournet was relieved of his command. Shown here are sailors from *Provence* disembarking for the landing at Pireaus.

Allies feared the possibility of modern Russian dreadnoughts and destroyers forming the nucleus of a new Central Powers fleet that could sortie from the Dardanelles and attack throughout the eastern Mediterranean. These fears came to naught as the Germans were able to bring only one Russian dreadnought into service in mid-October, only a month before the Armistice in the west was declared on 11 November 1918. However, the end of the war on the Western Front did not bring an end to the conflicts in the east. The dreadnought *Paris* and semi-dreadnought *Condorcet* saw brief service during the Greco-Turkish War, providing cover for the Greek landing at Smyrna in May 1919. Following the Allied occupation of Constantinople, which had begun on 12 November 1918, vessels of the *2e escadre* (2nd squadron) of the 1re Armée Navale were based there for operations in the Black Sea as part of the Allied intervention in the Russian Civil War; the Allies had occupied Odessa and Sevastopol in December 1918 in order to keep the ports out of Bolshevik hands. The dreadnoughts *France* and *Jean Bart* and the semi-dreadnoughts *Mirabeau* and *Vergniaud* patrolled the region from December 1918 to May 1919. On 8 February 1919 *Mirabeau* ran aground near Sevastopol during a squall; she was only refloated on 6 April after weeks of work to remove her fore primary turret, barbette and part of her armour. *Mirabeau* was towed back to Toulon in May, but the extent of the damage and the necessary reconstruction costs did not warrant the repair of the obsolescent vessel; she was decommissioned on 22 August and would be scrapped two years later.

On 16 April 1919 a Bolshevik offensive had pushed its way to the outskirts of Sevastopol and the Allied naval commander, Vice-Amiral Jean-François-Charles Amet, ordered the *France*, *Jean Bart*, *Vergniaud* and Greek pre-dreadnought *Kilkis* to bombard the Bolshevik lines. After a ceasefire was arranged between the Allies and the Bolsheviks, the weary French crews, most of whom had not been on French soil for several years, were given the false impression that they would finally be returning home. This was not the case, as Amet was determined to keep the Bolsheviks out of Sevastopol; he was not aware how low the morale of his battleship crews had sunk after years of frustration and inactivity. Three days later a mutiny broke out among 200 sailors aboard *France*; its leaders demanded better food and working conditions, an end to the Marine Nationale's involvement in the Russian Civil War and an immediate return of all French warships in the Black Sea to France. The last demand was the one insisted upon by the majority of the mutineers, who were affected by homesickness, war weariness and scepticism of the

White Russian cause. The mutiny spread to *Jean Bart* and on the following day to *Mirabeau* and *Vergniaud*. Red flags appeared on the vessels periodically throughout the mutiny, but the majority of mutineers made it clear to their officers that they were not Bolsheviks and were not interested in any revolutionary movements. While protests continued until 22 April there were no acts of aggression towards officers during the mutiny. By 22 April the mutineers aboard *Jean Bart*, *Mirabeau* and *Vergniaud* had settled back into their routines, refusing to follow the leads of the radical ringleaders.

There was still discontent aboard *France*, but on the following day Amiral Amet decided to sail his flagship back to French waters. The other ships would follow on 5 May after the Allied evacuation of Sevastopol. Mutinies also took place aboard *Voltaire* in Bizerte and *Provence* in Toulon in June 1919 pending departures to the east. These mutinies were likewise put down, but the involvement of the battleships of the Marine Nationale in the Russian Civil War was at an end. It was an inglorious conclusion to five years of demoralizing and idle service.

Mess time aboard *Lorraine*. Cramped living conditions and poor-quality food along with boredom from long periods of inactivity were some of the reasons which led to the April 1919 mutiny aboard French battleships at Sevastopol. (Author's collection)

The dreadnoughts and semi-dreadnoughts of the Marine Nationale never fought the enemy they had been developed to counter, the combined battlefleet of the Triple Alliance. Italy's about-face into the Allied camp and the k.u.k. Kriegsmarine's campaign of Kleinkrieg left France's battlefleet, ironically by 1914 the most powerful concentration of capital ships in the Mediterranean, without a clear mission. The refusal of the French and Italian admiralties to effectively conduct joint operations as allies forced both navies to operate their 'own forces' on patrol and interception duties, explaining the reason for the long-term stationing of the 1re Armée Navale in the Ionian Sea – resulting in the demoralizing idling among the battleship crews. During World War I the Marine Nationale lost 40 per cent of its effective strength and the near bankruptcy of the French state at the end of the conflict meant that funding for new construction would be minimal at best. The lack of funds and the inactivity of the battlefleet during the war led the Marine Nationale to prioritize the construction of new destroyers and cruisers before any new battleship construction.

Cover of a September 1922 issue of *Le Petit Journal* showing the loss of the Courbet class dreadnought *France*, which struck an uncharted rock in Quiberon Bay on the night of 18 July 1922. (Photo by Leemage/UIG via Getty Images)

It was France's signing of the Washington Naval Treaty of 1922, which limited the Marine Nationale's capital warship tonnage to 175,000 tons, that put an end to any post-war resumption of the 1912 Statut Naval. The remaining vessels of the Danton class – *Condorcet*, *Diderot* and *Voltaire* (*Vergniaud* was decommissioned in June 1921 owing to the poor condition of her machinery and scrapped in 1928) – were assigned to the *Division Navale de la Manche et de la mer du Nord* (Naval Division of the Channel and the North Sea) at Brest until early 1927, when they were sent to Toulon to serve as training vessels. *Diderot* and *Voltaire* were both decommissioned in 1937; the former was broken up that year while the latter was scuttled in Quiberon Bay in Brittany

Le Petit Journal illustré

Le Naufrage du Croiseur « France »

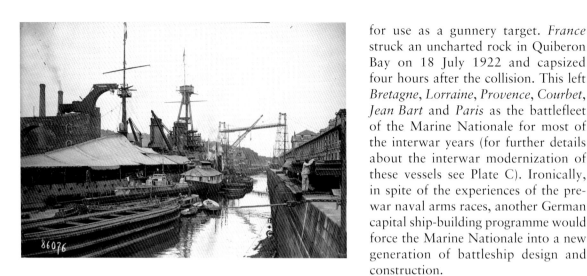

for use as a gunnery target. *France* struck an uncharted rock in Quiberon Bay on 18 July 1922 and capsized four hours after the collision. This left *Bretagne, Lorraine, Provence, Courbet, Jean Bart* and *Paris* as the battlefleet of the Marine Nationale for most of the interwar years (for further details about the interwar modernization of these vessels see Plate C). Ironically, in spite of the experiences of the pre-war naval arms races, another German capital ship-building programme would force the Marine Nationale into a new generation of battleship design and construction.

Paris undergoing modernization at the Arsenal de Brest in 1923. Note the new tripod mast. (Author's collection)

FAST BATTLESHIPS OF THE MARINE NATIONALE

Dunkerque class

During the negotiations which led to the final version of the Washington Naval Treaty of 1922, the French won an important concession. One of the conditions of the treaty demanded a ten-year moratorium on capital ship construction among all signatories, but the British argued for two modern 35,000-ton battleships (the Nelson class) to be constructed immediately to counter newer and more powerful American and Japanese battleships just entering service. The French and the Italians, whose existing battleships were armed only with 305mm and 340mm primary guns (compared to the larger 15in and 16in newer battleships of the British, Americans and Japanese), made a similar protest and were each granted the opportunity to lay down a new 35,000-ton capital ship

Strasbourg under construction at the Ateliers et Chantiers de Penhoët yards. (Author's collection)

in both 1927 and 1929. The leadership of both the Marine Nationale and the Regia Marina decided that they would utilize this 70,000 tons of new capital ship tonnage on any combination of designs, provided that a single ship did not exceed 35,000 tons. The Service technique des constructions navales worked on several preliminary 17,500-ton to 35,000-ton battlecruiser designs throughout the 1920s, but the Marine Nationale was inclined to pick a design from the lower end of the tonnage range. There were no naval yards with graving docks large enough to build a 35,000-ton warship in France and the cost of developing one would take funds away from cruiser and destroyer construction. The unveiling of Germany's 280mm gun-armed Deutschland class *Panzerschiff* project in 1928 was an unwelcome revelation to the Marine Nationale, but it brought some degree of clarity to what requirements would be needed in its next class of capital ship. What was needed was a warship which outgunned and was faster than the German *Panzerschiffe* while also having enough protection to counter their 280mm primary guns; at the same time such a vessel could easily counter the Trento and Zara class heavy cruisers built and being developed for the Regia Marina.

By 1930 the Service technique des constructions navales had developed a 23,333-ton *Croiseur de Bataille* (battlecruiser) design which mounted eight 305mm guns and had an armoured belt with a maximum thickness of 230mm. At the time the Marine Nationale considered the displacement to be key, because it would allow the construction of three identical ships under the terms of the Washington Naval Treaty. Eventually both the Parlement and the Conseil supérieur de la Marine wanted a vessel which was better armed

Crew of *Dunkerque* relaxing fore. The quadruple primary turrets were a weight-saving design measure utilized only by the French Dunkerque, Richelieu and British King George V class battleships, all designed within the limitations of the Washington Naval Treaty. (Author's collection)

and better protected, which resulted in a 26,500-ton design which was finalized in early 1932. Primary armament now consisted of eight newly developed 330mm/50 Modèle guns and the thickness of the armoured belt was increased to 250mm, all while maintaining a maximum speed of 30 knots. While the increased tonnage allowed for only two ships to be built, this new design was more than a match for the new vessels of the Deutschland class, but it also carried a more powerful armament, was better protected and was significantly faster than the Regia Marina's Conte di Cavour and Andrea Doria class battleships – and French graving docks could accommodate the size of the design. At the time it seemed like an ideal solution given the two potential rivals and the funding and logistical restrictions faced by the Marine Nationale. In December 1931 the Parlement approved funding for a single capital ship of the 26,500-ton design and granted funding for a sister ship in June 1934. On 24 December 1932 the Marine Nationale's first capital ship contracted in almost 20 years, *Dunkerque*, was laid down in the Arsenal de Brest. She was launched on 2 October 1935 and commissioned on 15 April 1937. Her sister *Strasbourg*, contracted from Ateliers et Chantiers de Saint-Nazaire Penhoët, was laid down on 25 November 1934, launched on 12 December 1936 and commissioned on 15 September 1938. Both ships appeared identical, but *Strasbourg* incorporated several design alterations, primarily increased protection, which gave the vessel a heavier tonnage.

Dunkerque class specifications

Dimensions	length: 215m; beam: 31.1m; draught: 9.8m
Full Displacement	*Dunkerque* – 35,500 tons; *Strasbourg* – 36,380 tons
Ship's Complement	1,431 men
Armament	eight Canon de 330mm/50 Modèle 31 guns in two quadruple turrets (330mm/50 gun had a range at 35 degrees elevation of 41,700m, could penetrate 342mm of armour at 23,000m with a 560kg armour-piercing shell and had an elevation range of -5 to 35 degrees; 100 rounds were carried per gun and 1–2 rounds could be fired per minute); 16 Canon de 130mm/45 Modèle 1935 dual-purpose secondary guns in three quadruple and two double turrets (130mm/45 gun had a range at 45 degrees elevation of 20,800m firing a 32.1kg high-explosive shell and had an elevation range of -10 to 75 degrees in a dual-purpose turret; 400 rounds were carried per gun and ten to 12 rounds could be fired per minute); eight (*Strasbourg*) and ten (*Dunkerque*) Canon de 37mm/50 Modèle 1925 anti-aircraft guns in four and five CAD Mle 1933 double turrets respectively (37mm/50 gun had a range at 45 degrees elevation of 5,000m and had an elevation of -15 to 80 degrees; 1,000 rounds were carried per gun and 15 to 21 rounds could be fired per minute); 32 mitrailleuse Hotchkiss de 13.2mm modèle 1929 machine guns in eight quadruple anti-aircraft mounts (guns were fed from 30-round box clips and had a rate of fire of 450 rounds per minute)
Machinery	four Parsons geared turbines, fired by six Indret boilers, producing up to 112,500 shaft horsepower and driving four screws up to a maximum speed of 30 knots
Maximum Range	16,416 nautical miles at 17 knots
Protection	armoured belt: *Dunkerque* – 225mm at the top tapering to 125mm at the bottom, *Strasbourg* – 283mm at the top tapering to 125mm at the bottom; conning tower: 270mm; barbettes: *Dunkerque* – 310mm, *Strasbourg* – 340mm; turrets: *Dunkerque* – 330mm on front, 345mm on the rear, 250mm on the sides and 150mm on the top, *Strasbourg* – 360mm on front, 355mm on the rear, 250mm on the sides and 160mm on top; armoured deck: 115–130mm
Aircraft	three Loire 130 flying boats launched from one catapult

Richelieu class

In October 1933 the Regia Marina, after holding off on capital ship construction since the signing of the Washington Naval Treaty in order to observe warship developments abroad, decided to drastically rebuild and modernize its Conte di Cavour class battleships; primary armament

E DUNKERQUE CLASS BATTLESHIP

In terms of aesthetics, *Dunkerque* and *Strasbourg* were to capital ship design as *Normandie* was to ocean liner design – elegant, streamlined and definitively modern. An immediately noticeable design anomaly compared to previous battleship designs were the two quadruple primary turrets, both located fore; never had a battleship been equipped with quadruple turrets and only one prior design, the British Nelson class, had all of its primary guns located fore with none aft. Each quadruple turret was actually two self-contained twin turrets mounted side-by-side. By concentrating four twin turrets into two quadruple turrets, the lack of additional turret structures, barbettes and protecting armour allowed for a 27.6 per cent weight reduction over a design which had four separate twin turrets. This weight reduction allowed for the use of heavier 330mm guns as opposed to the previously planned 305mm guns. The location of both turrets fore was due to unique tactical considerations. Intended as *Croiseur de Bataille*, the primary adversaries of the Dunkerque class were anticipated to be the German Panzerschiffe or German or Italian cruisers. Since combat with these vessels was likely to be a running pursuit, it made sense that all primary guns should be located in an offensive position. The lack of primary turrets aft allowed for the installation of an aircraft catapult and facilities that would not be susceptible to blast damage from heavy guns. The Dunkerque class capital ships were the first to have purposely designed aviation equipment and facilities, the aircraft intended to scout for enemy vessels (particularly fast cruisers and other commerce raiders) and to assist in gunnery spotting. The Dunkerque class was protected according to the all-or-nothing armour scheme, first implemented by the United States Navy's Nevada class battleships. The 225mm armoured belt was inclined at an 11.3 degree angle, giving it the effective resistance of 283mm of armour plate against shell hits.

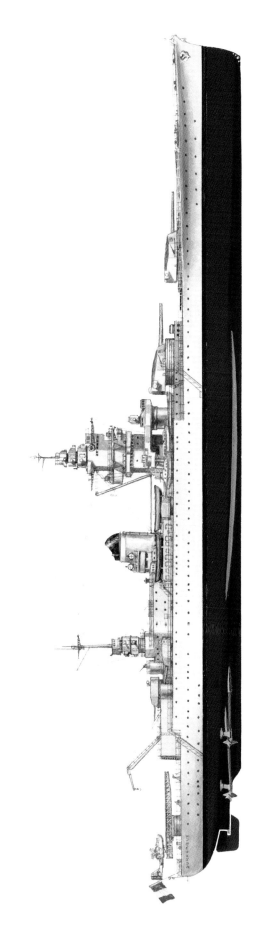
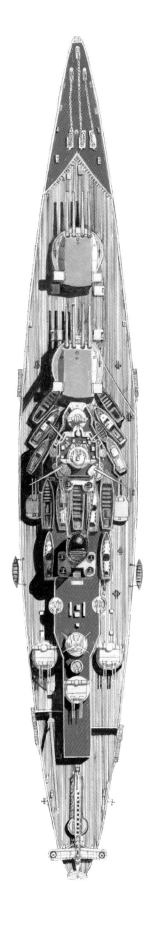

Richelieu after being launched at the Arsenal de Brest on 17 January 1939. (Photo by The LIFE Picture Collection/Getty Images)

would include ten heavier 320mm guns and new powerplants would give a maximum speed of 27 knots. The Andrea Doria class battleships would be likewise updated upon the completion of the Conte di Cavour class, giving the Regia Marina four capital ships with similar capabilities to the Dunkerques without any of its 'new' capital ship tonnage being utilized. Nine months later Mussolini's government announced its decision to construct two 35,000-ton fast battleships armed with 381mm guns, vessels designed to counter both the Dunkerques and the modernized Royal Navy battleships of the Queen Elizabeth and Revenge classes. Both of these developments abruptly gave the Regia Marina a decided advantage in its capital ship strength and threatened to throw off the balance of power in the Mediterranean. The Service technique des constructions navales was immediately tasked with the development of a 35,000-ton battleship design, which would mount eight/ nine 380mm or 406mm guns, have a maximum speed of 30 knots and be as heavily protected as possible. Designers were told to use the Dunkerque class design as a basis in order to save time and a design was approved by the Conseil Supérieur de la Marine Nationale in August 1935. Funding for a new vessel came quickly and both the Parlement and Marine Nationale agreed that construction should begin immediately.

The Marine Nationale was supposed to wait until the beginning of 1937 before starting any new capital ship construction outside of the tonnage permitted by the Washington Naval Treaty, since the French government had agreed to a clause in the subsequent London Naval Treaty of 1930 pushing back new capital ship construction for another five years. However, the Anglo-German Naval Agreement, signed in June 1935 and without the knowledge or involvement of the French government, radically altered the Marine Nationale's strategic planning. Germany was allowed by Great Britain to once again develop capital ships and legitimized the construction of the Scharnhorst class battleships, the first of which had already been laid down the previous month. Facing new battleship construction in both Germany and Italy and feeling that it could not rely upon Great Britain as a consistent ally, the French government deemed it a military necessity to openly violate the time constraints of the 1930 treaty. The first vessel of the Marine Nationale's new battleship class, *Richelieu*, was laid down on 10 October 1935 in the Arsenal de Brest graving dock vacated by Dunkerque only eight days before. The dock was not long enough to accommodate *Richelieu*'s full length, so the centre 197m section of the ship was constructed there while the 43m bow and 8m stern sections were added later in a longer fitting-out dock. Despite feeling betrayed by the British in 1935, the French government agreed to sign the Second London Naval Treaty the following year in an effort to forestall a threatening Continental naval arms race. This treaty compelled its signatories to continue to limit the maximum tonnage of a capital ship to 35,000 tons, which the French agreed to in spite of Italy's refusal to sign the treaty. This Italian action did prompt the Parlement to approve the purchase of a second Richelieu class battleship at the end of

May 1936 and *Jean Bart* was laid down in the new Ouvrage Caquot shipbuilding facility in the Ateliers et Chantiers de la Loire yards in Saint-Nazaire on 12 December 1936. Two more vessels of the Richelieu class were planned after the Marine Nationale learned of the laying down of the Bismarck class battleships in Germany in the second half of 1936, but the new French battleships were not authorized until May 1938 owing to the necessity to launch *Richelieu* and *Jean Bart* in order to free up the only suitable construction docks. *Richelieu* was launched on 17 January 1939 and commissioned on 1 April 1940, while *Jean Bart* was launched on 6 March 1940; neither was completely finished by the time of the French surrender in June 1940 and *Jean Bart* was not formally commissioned until after

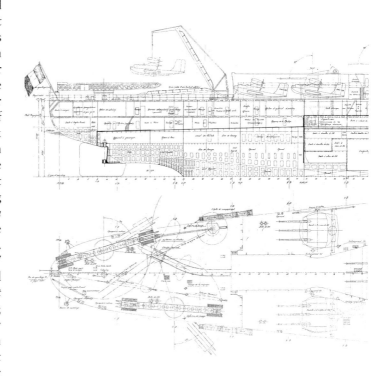

Design blueprint of *Richelieu*'s aviation facilities aft. These would be removed during *Richelieu*'s refit in New York in 1943 and the space used to mount a number of anti-aircraft batteries. (Author's collection)

the war on 1 August 1949. Of the third and fourth planned members of the Richelieu class, *Clemenceau* was laid down in Brest after *Richelieu* was launched, but it was only 10 per cent complete by June 1940; *Gascogne* never got beyond the drawing board.

Richelieu class specifications (for *Richelieu*, June 1940)

Dimensions	length: 247.85m; beam: 33.08m; draught: 9.9m
Full Displacement	44,698 tons
Ship's Complement	1,569 men
Armament	eight Canon de 380mm/45 Modèle 1935 guns in two quadruple turrets (380mm/45 gun had a range at 35 degrees elevation of 41,700m, could penetrate 393mm of side armour at 22,000m with a 884kg armour-piercing shell and had an elevation range of 5 to 35 degrees; 104 rounds were carried per gun and 1–2 rounds could be fired per minute); nine Canon de 152mm/55 Modèle 1930 dual-purpose secondary guns in three triple turrets (152mm/55 gun had a range at 45 degrees elevation of 24,200m firing a 47kg anti-aircraft shell and had an elevation range of -6.5 to 75 degrees in a dual-purpose turret; 400 rounds were carried per gun and five rounds could be fired per minute); 12 Canon de 100mm/45 Modèle 1930 anti-aircraft guns in six Model 1931 double turrets (100mm/45 gun had a range at 45 degrees elevation of 15,900m with a 13.5kg shell and had an elevation range of -10 to 80 degrees; 400 rounds were carried per gun and ten rounds could be fired per minute); eight Canon de 37mm/50 CAIL Modèle 1933 anti-aircraft guns in four twin CAD Mle 1933 mountings (similar characteristics to the 37mm/50 Modèle 1925 guns of the Dunkerque class); 20 mitrailleuse Hotchkiss de 13.2mm modèle 1929 machine guns in four quadruple and two twin anti-aircraft mounts
Machinery	four Parsons geared turbines, fired by six Sural-Indret boilers, producing up to 150,000 shaft horsepower and driving four screws up to a maximum speed of 30.31 knots
Maximum Range	10,000 nautical miles at 12 knots
Protection	armoured belt: 330mm; conning tower: 350mm; barbettes: 405mm; turrets: 430mm on front, 250mm on the rear, 300mm on the sides and 170mm on the top; armoured deck: 150mm to 170mm
Aircraft	three Loire 130 flying boats launched from two catapults

KEY

1. Loire 130 flying boats
2. Canon de 152mm/55 Modèle 1930 dual-purpose guns
3. 380mm fire control director
4. 152mm fire control director
5. 152mm fire control director
6. 380mm fire control director
7. Admiral's bridge
8. Canon de 380mm/45 Modèle 1935 guns
9. Turret I firing chamber
10. Turret I working chamber
11. Turret I upper handling room
12. Turret I lower handling room
13. Canon de 100mm/45 Modèle 1930 antiaircraft guns
14. Canon de 37mm/50 CAIL Modèle 1933 antiaircraft guns
15. Aircraft hanger

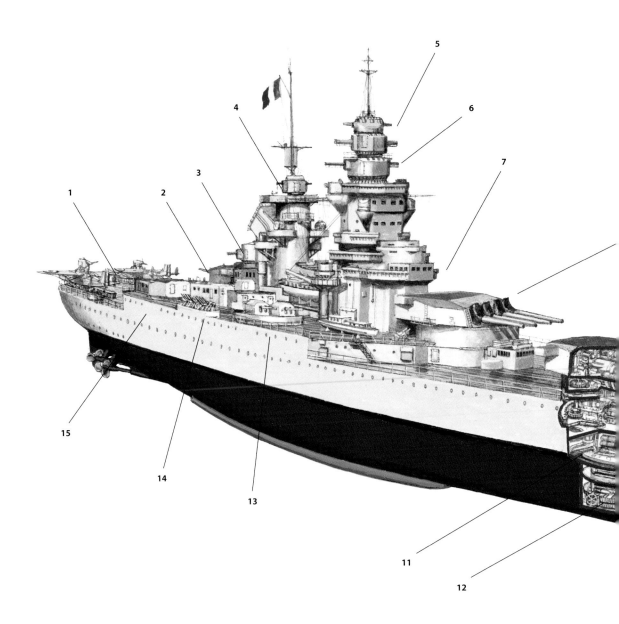

F RICHELIEU CLASS BATTLESHIP

The *Conseil Supérieur de la Marine* originally intended the vessels of the Richelieu class to be armed with eight or nine 406mm guns, but designers quickly determined that such guns would be too heavy for an adequately protected and fast battleship of 35,000 tons. Eight 380mm guns were decided upon, using the same weight-saving quadruple turret arrangement as in the Dunkerques. An armoured bulkhead separated each twin-gun mounting inside the quadruple turrets, so that if one side was damaged, the other could continue operation. For this same reason each side of the quadruple turrets were supplied by their own separate and contained ammunition and powder magazines. The quadruple turrets were also spaced further apart from each other compared with other battleships in order to reduce the risk of a magazine explosion disabling both primary turrets. The Dunkerque class's pioneering experimentation with dual-purpose (anti-ship/long-range anti-aircraft) secondary armament was continued with the Richelieu class, but the 130mm guns of the Dunkerques were thought to be inadequate for use against warships. Fifteen 152mm guns in five triple turrets, three aft and two amidships, were planned, but the low rate of fire of the 152mm gun (5rpm) compelled designers in 1939 to replace the amidships secondary turrets with twelve 100m twin-gun mounts. The Richelieu class possessed the same *caisson blindé* (box shielded) protection scheme as the Dunkerques but overall increased armour thickness as the additional tonnage allowed; the tonnage devoted to armour protection in the class accounted for over 39 per cent of each vessel's total weight, a higher protection ratio than any other battleship design in Europe at the time with the exception of the Bismarck class. A major design challenge was how to propel such a heavily armed and armoured vessel at a maximum speed of 30 knots within the 35,000-ton weight restriction. This was innovatively solved by installing experimental Sural-Indret pressure-fired boilers which produced significantly more steam per cubic metre than conventional boilers. Only six Sural-Indret boilers were installed in the Richelieu class (compared to eight conventional boilers in the Vittorio Veneto class and 12 in the Bismarck class) but these allowed the four turbines to generate 150,000hp, producing a maximum speed of 30.31 knots (compared to 128,200hp and 30 knots for *Vittorio Veneto* and 148,120hp and 30 knots for *Bismarck*). The amount of horsepower produced by the propulsion unit of the Richelieu class would not be surpassed in another battleship until the introduction of the much larger American Iowa class. Shown here is *Richelieu* in her 1940 configuration.

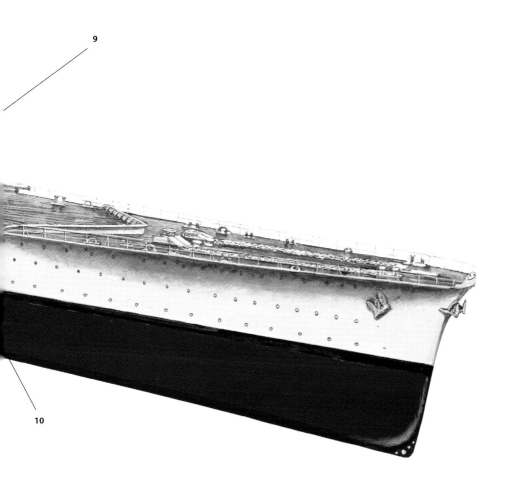

FRENCH BATTLESHIP OPERATIONS 1939–45

Operation *Catapult*, 3–7 July 1940

The first nine months of World War II were relatively uneventful for the Marine Nationale, largely owing to Italy's initial declaration of neutrality. *Dunkerque* and *Strasbourg* formed the nucleus of the new *Force de Raid*, a squadron of fast warships based at Brest, which was tasked with hunting down German Panzerschiffe conducting commerce raiding cruises in the Atlantic. Both vessels participated in a handful of Atlantic patrols in conjunction with warships of the Royal Navy, but they did not encounter any German raiders. By the spring of 1940 the growing threat of an Italian entry into the war alongside Germany compelled the Marine Nationale to base the Force de Raid in Algeria so that it could be well located to deal with potential threats in the Mediterranean and Atlantic; in late April *Dunkerque* and *Strasbourg* arrived at the naval base at Mers el-Kébir. The Bretagne class battleships participated in several convoy escort missions during the first months of the war and were also dispatched to the Mediterranean in May 1940; *Bretagne* and *Provence* joined the elements of the Force de Raid based at Mers el-Kébir, while *Lorraine* was sent to Alexandria to join Force X, a French squadron operating with the Royal Navy's Mediterranean Fleet. *Courbet* and *Paris*, both of which had served as gunnery training vessels since 1931, were once again made operational at Brest in May 1940. Late May and early June 1940, however, saw the rapid defeat of the French and British armies in northern France, and the German *Wehrmacht* marched into Paris on 14 June. Four days later the commander of the Marine Nationale, *Amiral de la Flotte* François Darlan, ordered all operational French naval vessels to sail to French North Africa or other ports outside of metropolitan France. *Richelieu* sailed out of Brest in the early morning of 19 June and proceeded to Dakar in French West Africa, arriving there on 23 June. At the same time the incomplete *Jean Bart* made her way out of St Nazaire and came under air attack by three German bombers while manoeuvring out of the River Loire, but reached Casablanca three days later. *Paris* sailed to Plymouth on 18 June, while *Courbet* fled to Portsmouth two days later.

On 21 June the French government entered into armistice negotiations with the Germans; one of the armistice articles demanded that French warships return to their peacetime ports in order to be disarmed and placed under German control. The French negotiators requested that the vessels of the French fleet disarm and remain in metropolitan or African ports under control of the French government after the armistice, a request which the Germans were willing to grant after the armistice was signed. Adolf Hitler personally granted this as he was eager to keep vessels of the Martine Nationale from continuing to fight alongside the British. On 22 June the Franco-German Armistice was formalized with the above article regarding the disposition of French warships intact and Darlan ordered the return to metropolitan or North African ports of French military

One of the Dunkerque class battleships photographed underway by one of its Loire 130 flying boats. The first months of World War II found *Dunkerque* and *Strasbourg* in the Atlantic, attempting to hunt down the German Panzerschiffe, which they themselves were designed to counter. (Author's collection)

and merchant vessels which had sought refuge in British ports. To the British it appeared that the Marine Nationale was about to be handed over to Germany, as the British government and Royal Navy had not been informed about the German decision to allow the French to keep control of their warships. This was due to communications difficulties between the British and French leadership in the wake of the armistice, caused by the withdrawal of British diplomats and military missions from France and the movements of the French government following its evacuation from Paris. Despite

Maréchal Phillippe Petain and Amiral François Darlan of the Vichy French regime. Winston Churchill and the British War Cabinet were reluctant to believe the Vichy chiefs' promises that the vessels of the *Marine Nationale* would never fall into German hands. This mistrust led to over two years of sporadic naval conflict between the *Marine Nationale* and the naval forces of the Allies. (Photo by Gabriel Hackett/Archive Photos/Getty Images)

Darlan's earlier promises to the Royal Navy that French warships would be scuttled if the Germans attempted to take control of them, Prime Minister Winston Churchill and the British War Cabinet resolved on 27 June that it was imperative that the vessels of the Marine Nationale, particularly its capital units, did not fall into Axis hands. The addition of *Dunkerque* and *Strasbourg* alone to either of the Axis navies (although the ability of the Axis to equip and crew any French vessels without considerable delay and effort was negligible) would offset the slight numerical advantage in capital ships possessed by the Royal Navy at that time. Churchill and the War Cabinet subsequently authorized Operation *Catapult*, the neutralization of French naval forces in British ports and capital units in French colonial ports; the date of the operation was set for 3 July. Ironically the first ship-on-ship combat seen by France's battleships would be against vessels of the Royal Navy.

As dawn broke on 3 July lookouts in Mers el-Kébir discovered a sizeable British squadron assembling offshore. In the late afternoon of 2 July, Admiral Sir James Somerville had sailed from Gibraltar with Force H (the battleships *Hood*, *Resolution* and *Valiant*, aircraft carrier *Ark Royal*, light cruisers *Arethusa* and *Enterprise* and 11 destroyers) with orders to deliver the following terms to Vice-Amiral Marcel Gensoul, commander of the Force du Raid: sail his warships to British ports, either to fight on alongside Great Britain or to be disarmed and interned; sail his vessels with reduced crews under British control to the French West Indies or the United States where they would be disarmed and retained for the remainder of the war; or French crews to scuttle their own ships. If these options were refused then Force H would be tasked with sinking Gensoul's warships. In Mers el-Kébir at the time were *Dunkerque*, *Strasbourg*, *Bretagne*, *Provence*, the seaplane carrier *Commandant Teste* and six destroyers. After receiving the British terms from a representative sent by Somerville, Gensoul initially stated that his vessels would never fall into German hands, but that he would also retaliate against any British aggression against his squadron. Gensoul continued the negotiations in the hope that this confrontation could be peacefully resolved, but also to buy time in order to contact Amiral Darlan about the situation as well as prepare his vessels and the harbour's defences for battle, should the situation arise. The warships, coastal batteries (consisting of three old 240mm guns at Fort Canastel and four 194mm guns at Fort Jebel Santon) and aircraft at nearby airfields had all begun the process of demobilization in accordance with the terms of the Franco-German Armistice. Protection

from the coastal batteries would be necessary as Gensoul's battleships were moored with their sterns against the mole (running north to south), facing away from sea; *Dunkerque* and *Strasbourg*, with all of their primary guns fore, would be unable to defend themselves as they had to exit the harbour from the south and then the east. When Amiral Darlan learned about the situation at Mers el-Kébir, he ordered all available French warships in the western Mediterranean to proceed immediately to Gensoul's assistance. By late afternoon, however, the British admiralty had learned of the French reinforcements en route to Mers el-Kébir and pressed Somerville to resolve the standoff. With Gensoul still refusing the British terms, at 16:35 *Ark Royal* began flying off a strike group and Somerville's battleships positioned themselves to open fire.

At 16:56 the British began their attack. Gensoul ordered his battleships to immediately get underway and proceed to sea in the following order: *Strasbourg, Dunkerque, Provence* and *Bretagne*. His six destroyers were instructed to sail independently and get out of the harbour as quickly as possible. *Strasbourg* began to move out immediately and avoided being struck by any British shells during the attack. *Dunkerque* and *Provence* were hit as they attempted to get underway and both were beached along the coast. Before she was able to proceed *Bretagne* was hit by two shells which triggered a series of explosions in her stern, causing her to capsize ten minutes later (see Plate G for additional details of the battle). At 17:12 Somerville called a halt to the attack; by this time he was receiving signals from Gensoul to cease fire and the fire from the 240mm batteries at Fort Canastel was beginning to bracket his vessels. At 17:10 *Strasbourg* cleared the harbour channel along with the other five destroyers from Mers el-Kébir; the French battleship was not initially observed by the British. Somerville had moved out further to the west owing to fire from onshore batteries, and smoke from explosions aboard *Bretagne* and the destroyer *Mogador* (whose stern was blown off by a 15in shell in the harbour channel during the bombardment) provided unexpected cover. Furthermore, the British did not expect any French vessels to leave the harbour quickly, as Fairey Swordfish torpedo bombers from *Ark Royal* had dropped five magnetic mines across the entry channel earlier that day at 12:30. Gensoul, however, anticipating the need for a hasty escape, had the channel swept during the afternoon and had the harbour booms opened, something which was not observed by the British. Upon exiting the channel, the French destroyers *Lynx* and *Tigre* proceeded to attack the only British vessel nearby, the destroyer *Wrestler*, which was driven off and made smoke to cover the British capital ships further to the west. Captain Louis Collinet of *Strasbourg* then ordered his vessel to proceed to the north-east along the coast at full speed, hoping he could evade the British and make for Toulon.

Collinet managed to proceed for almost half an hour before the British turned to pursue him. Somerville had discounted earlier aerial reconnaissance reports of *Strasbourg*'s escape, but finally turned eastward with *Hood*, *Arethusa*, *Enterprise* and several destroyers at 17:38. *Strasbourg* could only make 28 knots due to splinter damage to the air intakes on her funnel, but fortunately she was out of effective firing range of *Hood*'s guns and the British battlecruiser, badly in need of a refit, could only make 27 knots. Somerville ordered *Ark Royal* to mount air attacks against the escaping *Strasbourg* and the first of these, consisting of six Swordfish armed with bombs and four Blackburn Skua fighter escorts, arrived over the target at 18:45. The Swordfish achieved no hits, but at this time the British received an unpleasant surprise; several French Curtiss H-75 fighter aircraft arrived overhead and managed to shoot down a few of the British attackers. By 19:20 Collinet had managed to bring *Strasbourg* 25 miles ahead of her pursuers and Somerville's force was unable to close any distance; the French submarines out of Oran had drawn off several of the British destroyers, two of *Strasbourg*'s escorts had launched a long-range torpedo attack against *Hood* – forcing the British to take evasive action – and the sun was beginning to set. At 19:25 Somerville called off the pursuit and turned to the north-west. A group of torpedo-carrying Swordfish made one final attack on *Strasbourg* shortly after sunset at 19:55, but there were no hits. Under the cover of darkness Collinet turned his vessel northward and arrived in Toulon to a hero's welcome, with bands playing *le Marseillaise*, the following evening. Churchill was furious.

The British would have the last word in the Mers el-Kébir debacle, however. Somerville and Force H were back at Gibraltar preparing for an operation against the *Richelieu* at Dakar, but the War Cabinet ordered him to proceed again to Mers el-Kébir and finish off the *Dunkerque* after aerial reconnaissance could not ascertain the true level of damage to the warship. Force H put to sea on the evening of 5 July and arrived undetected 90 miles to the west of Oran in the early hours of the following morning. Back at Mers el-Kébir the French warships had largely been evacuated and only caretaker crews and damage-control parties had been left aboard. In an effort to avoid subsequent attacks, Gensoul had radioed Somerville on the evening of 3 July that his vessels were out of action and crews would be kept ashore. At 05:15 on 6 July the French awoke to the sound of 12 Swordfish from *Ark Royal* roaring in for a low-level torpedo attack. Amazingly none of the torpedoes hit *Dunkerque*, but one hit and sank the patrol boat *Terre-Neuve* which was moored along the battleship's starboard side. A subsequent torpedo hit the sunken *Terre-Neuve*'s stern, setting off a number of depth charges, and the resulting explosion wrenched apart the starboard hull underneath *Dunkerque*'s second primary turret. Her main 330mm magazine would probably have exploded, completely destroying the ship, but fortunately it had

Dunkerque beached at Mers el-Kébir following the British attacks. (Author's collection)

Vichy French propaganda poster attacking a 'treacherous' Churchill following the strikes at Mers el-Kébir and Dakar. (Photo by Bettmann/Contributor/Getty Images)

Paris photographed in Plymouth in 1941. *Paris* and *Courbet* were the only French battleships to fall under British control following Operation *Catapult*. (Naval History and Heritage Command NH 88985)

been flooded at the beginning of the attack. Nevertheless, *Dunkerque* remained immobilized at Mer el-Kébir until July 1941 and was unable to return to Toulon for full repairs until February 1942, owing to the almost constant state of combat throughout the western Mediterranean.

After the attacks at Mers el-Kébir, Churchill and the Royal Navy turned their attentions to the *Richelieu*. Except for an aborted journey to Casablanca, *Richelieu* had remained at anchor in the Bay of Dakar since she arrived in French West Africa on 23 June. Her primary batteries were made operational, but the loading systems inside the turrets were unfinished when she left Brest; a makeshift system was devised, but it took 15 minutes to reload the guns. The fire control system for the dual-purpose 152mm guns and 100mm anti-aircraft guns had not yet been installed either, hampering the vessel's ability to defend itself against aerial attack. Since the signing of the armistice, Captain Paul Jean Marzin, *Richelieu*'s commander, was wary of British intentions regarding his vessel. The British cruiser *Dorsetshire* had been shadowing *Richelieu*'s movements and kept a vigil off Dakar, just outside the range of the port's coastal batteries. Following the 3 July attack at Mers el-Kébir, Marzin anchored *Richelieu* behind the harbour's torpedo nets and surrounded the exposed rear flank of his vessel with lines of cargo ships commandeered from the port. On the afternoon of 7 July a British task force, centred around the aircraft carrier *Hermes* and the heavy cruisers *Australia* and *Dorsetshire*, appeared off Dakar; an ultimatum similar to that issued to Gensoul was sent to the French military authorities. Contre-Amiral Jean Baptiste Émile Plaçon, the naval commander for French West Africa, refused to acknowledge the ultimatum and Captain Marzin made preparations to sail out the following morning and drive off the British. During the night a small group of British marines from *Hermes* secretly penetrated the harbour in a motor launch and sank four depth charges along *Richelieu*'s stern. The depth charges failed to explode, but the marines escaped undetected. At dawn the next day six Swordfish from *Hermes* made a surprise torpedo attack against *Richelieu* despite Marzin's defensive measures. One of the torpedoes struck between the starboard propeller shafts and the explosion set off the depth charges from the earlier raid, amplifying the damage. Rapidly taking on water, Marzin moved *Richelieu* into the port where her stern settled on the shallow bottom. The British sailed away unscathed. Full repairs to *Richelieu*'s shafts could not be undertaken at Dakar and it was too dangerous to attempt to send her to an unoccupied French port in a crippled condition.

Not every incident in Operation *Catapult* involved combat. British boarding parties took control of *Paris* in Plymouth and *Courbet* in Portsmouth before dawn broke. Both battleships were secured quickly and without a fight; the French crews were taken by surprise as they had become accustomed to British liaison parties visiting their ships. In Alexandria Vice-Admiral Andrew Cunningham, commander of the Royal Navy's Mediterranean Fleet, presented Vice-Amiral René-Émile Godfroy, commander of Force X (*Lorraine*, the cruisers *Duquesne*, *Suffren*, *Tourville* and *Duguay-Trouin*, and three destroyers) similar terms which had been given to Gensoul at Mers el-Kébir. Eager to avoid bloodshed, Cunningham suggested that the French vessels discharge their fuel and maintain the status quo into the next day to allow for negotiations, an alternative which Godfroy accepted. After reports of the attack at Mers el-Kébir reached Alexandria, both admirals were ordered to attack each other. The last thing Cunningham wanted however was a battle to take place in the harbour which might cause damage to the port's facilities or result in wrecks of vessels blocking channels or anchorages. Godfroy realized the futility of his position as his vessels were stationary in a port and under the 15in guns of the battleships *Warspite*, *Malaya*, *Royal Sovereign* and

Lorraine at anchor in Alexandria during her three-year sequestration. (© IWM A 18293)

Ramilles. An agreement was worked out between the two admirals under which the French vessels would not be seized, but they would be disarmed, their complements reduced to caretaker crews and the breech-blocks of the guns would be removed and stored at the French consulate in Alexandria. Both Darlan and Churchill were irritated by this unauthorized détente, but it remained in place until 1943. Ironically, Operation *Catapult* proved to be the largest naval campaign involving the Marine Nationale during World War II and affected almost all of its battleships; only the unfinished *Jean Bart* at Casablanca was left unmolested by the British. In retrospect Operation *Catapult* proved to be an effective statement of Churchill's fierce determination to carry on the war, but at the time the only immediate beneficiary of the operation was Germany; the attacks had effectively forced a wedge between the British and the new *État Français*, colloquially known as Vichy France, and diplomatic relations between the two were severed on 8 July.

Richelieu and Operation *Menace*, 23–25 September 1940

Richelieu's encounters with the Royal Navy did not end with the aerial torpedo attack on 7 July. At the end of August 1940 most of French Equatorial Africa had declared its support for General Charles de Gaulle and his Free French government-in-exile, the *Conseil de défense de l'Empire*. De Gaulle believed he could convince the Vichy French authorities in Dakar to join his movement and Churchill decided to authorize a joint British-Free French expedition, code-named Operation *Menace*, to secure the port. The Royal Navy assembled a task force, Force M, under the command of Vice Admiral John Cunningham, made up of the battleships *Barham* and *Resolution*, the aircraft carrier *Ark Royal*, five cruisers, 17 destroyers and escorts, and troop ships carrying 6,400 British and French ground troops. On the morning of 23 September Force M arrived off Dakar undetected due to dense fog and Cunningham sent a flight of Swordfish torpedo bombers from *Ark Royal* over the port, dropping leaflets which urged the population to join the Free French cause. Dakar's naval commander, Contre-Amiral Marcel Landriau, refused to negotiate with De Gaulle or Cunningham and ordered the warships in the harbour (*Richelieu*, the cruisers *Georges Leygues* and *Montcalm*, and four destroyers) and the surrounding coastal batteries (five batteries mounting a total of nine 240mm/50 and eight 138mm guns) to prepare for battle. *Richelieu* was moored along a mole at the eastern end of the harbour; only one of her primary turrets and two secondary turrets were manned, as some of her gun crews were dispatched to assist the undermanned coastal batteries. Owing to the previous torpedo attack, *Richelieu* could not effectively get underway, but makeshift repairs had contained the flooding in the stern, allowing her to serve as a floating battery. By 09:00 Cunningham learned that the French warships in Dakar were preparing to get under way and he ordered his vessels to take up their firing positions.

At 11:05 *Barham* and *Resolution* began a 20-minute bombardment aimed at *Richelieu* with their 15in batteries. None of the British shells hit *Richelieu* and only minor splinter damage was sustained. *Richelieu* was unable to return fire with her operable 380mm turret, because she was moored facing northwards while the British were located to the south-east. Captain Marzin of *Richelieu* had a tug manoeuvre his vessel's stern away from the mole so he could bring his big guns to bear on the enemy, but by the time this was accomplished the British battleships had ceased firing, sailing off out of the range of Dakar's coastal batteries. Cunningham halted his bombardment in the hope that a peaceful outcome might still be achieved, but De Gaulle believed that a negotiated resolution was no longer possible and implored him and Churchill to abandon the mission. Churchill would have none of it, however, and demanded that Cunningham seize Dakar by force. Later that afternoon an amphibious landing was attempted to the east of Dakar, but it was aborted when determined artillery and machine-gun fire was encountered along the landing zone. During the evening of

G

THE BATTLE OF MERS EL-KÉBIR, 3 JULY 1940

After the bombardment of Mers el-Kébir began, *Dunkerque* and *Provence* immediately returned fire upon the British (some of *Provence's* guns being aimed between *Dunkerque's* masts) but their targeting was hampered by having to fire over a fort and terrain to their starboard. At 16:59 two 15in shells from the third British salvo struck *Bretagne* aft; one caused a massive explosion in the 340mm magazine between the two rear turrets and the other exploded in an engine room, knocking out communications and power throughout the ship. The hit to the magazine caused other successive explosions aft and *Bretagne* began to sink by the stern. Although *Strasbourg* got underway within moments following the opening of the British attack, *Dunkerque* did not slip her moorings until 17:00. Just as she began to turn to port three 15in shells from the same British salvo struck *Dunkerque* amidships and aft, damaging a boiler room, severing the rudder cables and knocking out the main switchboard, causing the loss of electrical power throughout the ship. Without power her turrets could not be trained and she was losing speed and the ability to easily manoeuvre from the other damage. *Dunkerque's* captain ordered her to be beached directly across the harbour. *Provence* could not get underway until *Dunkerque* had passed her, and she continued to fire on the British from her mooring position. While still stationary, *Provence* was hit aft at 17:03 by a 15in shell which started an internal fire and caused flooding. She managed to get underway, but the heat from the fire posed a threat to the aft magazines and her captain ordered their flooding as a precautionary measure. It was soon discovered that the flooding could not be controlled and her captain ordered *Provence* run aground to save her. While the crews of *Dunkerque* and *Provence* were assessing the damage, two 15in shells hit *Bretagne* amidships at 17:06, setting off a store of ready-to-use anti-aircraft munitions. Three minutes later *Bretagne* suddenly capsized and sank within 20 seconds, taking 1,012 men with her, roughly 85 per cent of her complement. Shortly after the British ceased firing *Dunkerque* ran aground at 17:13, followed by *Provence* further to the south. *Commandant Teste* received no direct hits, but remained in the harbour to rescue crewman from *Bretagne*. *Strasbourg* is shown here steaming past the seaplane tender *Commandant Teste* as explosions rock *Bretagne* aft.

23 September Cunningham resolved to neutralize Dakar's coastal defences and the warships in its harbour through aerial and naval bombardment on the following day. Meanwhile, in the port *Richelieu* had been manoeuvred into a better firing position, while the cruisers and destroyers took up positions in the outer harbour.

Although weather conditions on 24 September were still hazy, overall visibility had improved enough for Cunningham to deploy *Ark Royal*'s aircraft. At 07:13 six Skuas, each armed with 500lb bombs, made a glide bomb attack against *Richelieu*, but achieved only two near-misses. Another aerial attack was made against *Richelieu* at 09:10 when six Swordfish, each armed with four 250lb bombs, dive bombed the battleship, again only obtaining a few near-misses. By this time a Vichy French fighter patrol was over the harbour and the Curtiss H-75s, along with anti-aircraft fire from *Richelieu*, managed to shoot down three Swordfish and three escorting Skuas. Shortly after this air battle Cunningham's battleships and cruisers took up their bombardment positions to the south and Dakar's coastal batteries opened fire at 09:35. *Richelieu* targeted *Barham* and her Turret II fired its first full salvo at 09:40. Disaster immediately struck, however, when defective shells exploded in the two starboard guns, shattering the barrel of the inboard one and stripping a portion of the rifling in the outboard one. The port guns of Turret II resumed firing at 10:07 following an inspection, but a shell from one of *Richelieu*'s secondary turrets hit *Barham* in the bilge at 09:57. The British returned in the early afternoon and *Barham* opened fire on *Richelieu* at 13:05, with *Resolution* targeting one of the 240mm coastal batteries. Marzin had already ordered Turret II's remaining operational guns to open fire on the approaching British at 12:56 and he radioed the destroyer *Le Hardi* to make a smokescreen across the harbour. *Richelieu* achieved no hits against the British, but also suffered no hits during the bombardment. After only 15 minutes of action *Barham* had taken four hits from the 240mm batteries and Cunningham again withdrew at 13:20. That evening Marzin transferred the gunnery crew from the damaged Turret II to Turret I, and the night was spent making the turret operational.

Believing that the attacks on 24 September had caused more damage than they actually did, owing to faulty intelligence reports, Cunningham decided to again bombard Dakar's defences the following day. The French spotted the British approach shortly before 08:00. Once within range of its 380mm guns *Richelieu* opened fire against *Barham* at 08:58. As *Barham* and *Resolution* turned to return fire, lookouts spotted the wakes of four rapidly approaching torpedoes; at the approach of the British battleships, the Vichy submarine *Bévéziers* had sailed out of Dakar, manoeuvred into a firing position and launched four torpedoes shortly after 09:00. *Barham* managed to dodge the torpedoes, but one struck *Resolution* amidships on the port side, knocking out her port boiler room. As *Resolution* limped away under a smokescreen laid by two destroyers, *Barham* fired on *Richelieu* and managed to hit her with a 15in shell at 09:15; the shell struck amidships, but it failed to penetrate the armoured belt, causing minimal damage. *Richelieu's* Turret I continued its fire against *Barham* and one 380mm shell struck *Barham* aft, but it failed to cause serious damage. Two shells from one of *Richelieu's* secondary turrets also managed to hit the cruiser *Australia*. Given the severe damage to *Resolution* and the aggressive French defensive actions, Cunningham ceased the bombardment at 09:21 and called off Operation *Menace* by the end of the morning. The Allied failure at Dakar dealt a heavy blow to the prestige of De Gaulle and the Free French movement, and proved to be a personal embarrassment for Churchill. In the battle, Cunningham managed to cripple the destroyer *L'Audacieux* and sink two submarines while losing none of his own vessels, but his forces failed to sink, let along cripple *Richelieu*.

Jean Bart and Operation Torch, 8–10 November 1942

More than two years passed after Operation *Menace* before the battleships of the Marine Nationale saw further combat, and the next time one did it would be pitted against a different contender: the United States Navy. In the early autumn of 1942 the Americans and British planned to invade French North Africa to relieve pressure on British forces in Egypt. The resulting campaign, Operation *Torch*, was set to begin on 8 November 1942 with amphibious landings near Casablanca, Oran and Algiers. Throughout the early morning hours of 8 November reports started to trickle in to the Vichy naval commander in Casablanca, Vice-Amiral Frix Michelier, of Allied naval activity off the Moroccan and Algerian coasts, and at 05:00 Allied aircraft overflew the city, dropping pamphlets requesting cooperation with American forces. In Casablanca harbour Michelier had at his disposal the light cruiser *Primauguet* and seven operational destroyers; his most potent asset however was the still-incomplete *Jean Bart*. When the battleship escaped from St Nazaire only half her turbines and boilers were operational and only the outer two propellers had been mounted, giving her a maximum speed of only 12–14 knots. In terms of armament, only her primary Turret I had been completed and she lacked all of her 152mm secondary turrets, but an ersatz anti-aircraft arrangement was installed. Over the next two years in Casablanca *Jean Bart's* empty primary and secondary turret openings were cemented over and she was fitted with four 90mm dual-purpose guns and three 37mm, 14 13.2mm and one 8mm anti-aircraft guns. With the propulsion systems still incomplete, it would have been suicidal to send *Jean Bart* to sea, but she proved to be very useful as a powerful floating

American aerial reconnaissance photograph of Casablanca's inner harbour taken on 9 November 1942. *Jean Bart* and her operational primary turret can be seen at the far left of the photograph. (Library of Congress LC-USW33-017651-ZC)

battery. The United States Navy likewise realized the potential threat to their operations posed by *Jean Bart*'s 380mm guns. The American OSS (Office of Strategic Services, predecessor of the CIA) had been tracking the minimal construction work going on aboard the vessel for months and knew that one of her primary turrets was operational. The *Jean Bart* was thus one of the initial targets of American Task Force 34, commanded by Rear-Admiral Henry Hewitt and consisting of five aircraft carriers, three battleships, three heavy and four light cruisers, and 38 destroyers – all of which were supporting the landing of 35,000 ground troops under the command of Major-General George S. Patton.

At 07:04 the battleship *Massachusetts* and cruiser *Tuscaloosa* opened fire and *Jean Bart* responded four minutes later. At 07:10 17 Douglas SBD Dauntless dive bombers from the US aircraft carrier *Ranger*, having circled around the city waiting for the naval bombardment to commence, attacked *Jean Bart* and other French vessels in the harbour. One 500lb bomb struck near the port aircraft catapult and penetrated through several decks, while a near-miss along the quay by another bomb ruptured hull plating on the starboard side near the rear boiler room. At 07:08 *Jean Bart* targeted *Massachusetts* and fired four two-gun salvoes, but ceased firing at 07:19 when a smokescreen, laid by *Primauguet* and her escorts as they prepared to head out to sea, obscured the Americans. The gunfire from *Massachusetts* was initially inaccurate, but from 07:25 to 08:10 *Jean Bart* was struck by seven 16in shells from the American battleship. One 16in shell penetrated the armoured deck and exploded in one of the aft 152mm magazines, which fortunately for the French was empty. One ricocheted off the barbette of Turret I, but the impact jammed the turret in place. Another penetrated the quarterdeck and exploded in a ballast compartment just below the steering gear, resulting in flooding. The other 16in shells passed through lightly armoured sections of the ship or failed to explode, causing minimal damage. The Americans ceased their attack against *Jean Bart* at 08:35, believing the French battleship had been neutralized. This engagement would be one of only three battleship-on-battleship engagements fought by the United States Navy in the 20th century (others were the Second Naval Battle of Guadalcanal and the Battle of Surigao Strait). Throughout the morning and afternoon of 8 November *Jean Bart*'s crew patched up the damage from *Massachusetts*' bombardment and civilian contractors made Turret I operational again. *Jean Bart*'s commander, capitaine de vaisseau Émile Barthes, ordered that the turret remain in the position in which it was jammed so as not to let the Americans know it was again operational.

Jean Bart (identified by her tall superstructure) seen just above the buildings along a quay in Casablanca during the American bombardment. Vichy destroyers in the harbour are making smoke to obscure the battleship. (Photo by © Hulton-Deutsch Collection/CORBIS/ Corbis via Getty Images)

On 10 November Major General Patton began his march towards Casablanca. At 10:10 two French sloops and a patrol boat sortied from Casablanca to attack American ground forces marching along the coast. The French vessels were spotted by American aircraft and Admiral Hewitt's flagship, the heavy cruiser *Augusta*, and four destroyers closed in to intercept, opening fire at 11:25. *Jean Bart*, her gunnery crews having carefully tracked the movements of Hewitt's vessels, targeted *Augusta* and fired nine two-gun salvoes at the cruiser beginning at 11:41. The last three salvoes straddled *Augusta*, sending cascades of water over the cruiser's bridge and upper works, and she beat a hasty retreat behind a smokescreen. Hewitt ordered *Ranger*'s air group to launch an air strike against *Jean Bart*, and nine Dauntless dive bombers, armed this time with 1,000lb bombs, arrived over Casablanca at 14:58. One bomb penetrated the forecastle and exploded, blowing open a wide hole to starboard. Another bomb hit the quarterdeck near the starboard catapult near where a 500lb bomb and a 16in shell had struck two days earlier; the explosion tore open a broad section of the quarter deck and starboard hull in front of the catapult. Flooding from the second

Damage to *Jean Bart*'s starboard side aft near the aircraft catapult from a 500lb bomb from the American carrier strike of 10 November 1942. (Naval History and Heritage Command 80-G-31605)

bomb hit and firefighting efforts caused *Jean Bart*'s stern to settle on the harbor bottom later that evening. Ironically as the dive bombers were carrying out their assault against *Jean Bart*, Amiral Michelier received a message from Amiral Darlan in Algiers stating that he had negotiated a ceasefire with the Americans several hours before and ordered all Vichy forces in Africa to join the Allies; the battleship's term of service to the Vichy regime was at an end. Although the battleship had been hit by four aerial bombs, seven 16in shells and several near-misses, her 380mm guns still remained operational – and would be put to good use later in the war.

The collapse of Vichy France to the end of the war

Reacting swiftly to the Allied invasion of North Africa and Darlan's change of sides, the German High Command issued the execution of Operation *Anton*, the planned occupation of Vichy France, on 11 November 1942. At first the German High Command agreed not to occupy Toulon or seize the vessels of the Marine Nationale, provided that the French would defend themselves against any Allied attack, but in the early hours of 27 November Hitler ordered Operation *Lila*, the capture of Toulon and the intact seizure of French naval units there, to commence. At the time Toulon was home to the vessels of the *Forces de Haute Mer* (High Seas Forces), the main operational force of the Vichy fleet under the command of Amiral Jean de Laborde. This force consisted of *Strasbourg*, five cruisers and 13 destroyers. Also at Toulon were the vessels of the *Division des Écoles* (Training Division), including *Provence* (refloated and sailed to Toulon in November 1940) and the semi-dreadnought *Condorcet*, as well as vessels *en gardiennage d'Armistice* (under the guard of the Armistice), including *Dunkerque* (refloated and partially repaired at Mers el-Kébir before being sent to Toulon in January 1942). At 05:25 German panzers rolled through the naval base's main gate, its commanders taken by surprise. Fortunately for the French, the panzers got lost in the early morning darkness amid the numerous buildings, alleys and docks of the base. Upon learning of the German assault, Amiral de Laborde, aboard *Strasbourg*, sent out the order via radio and light signal for all vessels to scuttle immediately. Around 06:00 a panzer detachment finally located *Strasbourg*, but by that time her sea-cocks had been opened and she was in the process of settling on the harbour bottom. At 06:20 a warning siren sounded and scuttling charges began exploding throughout the ship, disabling her

guns and propulsion machinery. At the same time explosions tore through the *Strasbourg*, the captain of *Provence* ordered his vessel's sea-cocks opened as he attempted to delay the Germans; as the parley went on *Provence* began to list and then settled on the bottom before the Germans could intervene. Across the base in the Vauban graving docks there was only a minimal maintenance crew aboard *Dunkerque*, but it was aided by the fact that the Germans did not approach the vessel until 07:00; the crew was able to blow up the guns and disable the turbines.

Strasbourg shown settled on the harbour bottom following her scuttling at Toulon on 27 November 1942. A Loire 130 flying boat is in the foreground, while the cruiser *Colbert* still burns behind *Strasbourg*. (Photo by Klaus Wentzel/ ullstein bild via Getty Images)

Operation *Lila* was a failure for the Germans as 77 warships, around half of the Vichy navy, were scuttled. For the French, ironically this drastic action upheld agreements made to both Great Britain and Germany – that French warships would not fall into German hands and vice versa. As for the crews of the scuttled vessels, they experienced the same sentiments as German crews of the High Seas Fleet had 23 years earlier at Scapa Flow – honour tempered with bitter disappointment.

During the first half of 1943, Vichy-controlled French colonial territories, including the naval units stationed within them, joined the Allied cause and came under the control of the Free French government, reorganized as the *Comité français de Libération nationale* (French Committee of National Liberation) on 3 June 1943. *Lorraine* received a badly needed refit in Oran in December 1943. With a greatly improved anti-aircraft arrangement, *Lorraine* provided shore bombardment support during the invasion of southern France, code-named Operation *Dragoon*, in the latter half of August 1944. In late 1944 *Lorraine* was sent to Cherbourg to become the flagship of the French Naval Task Force, an all-French squadron which would provide shore bombardment for assaults on remaining German *Atlantikfestungen*, or Atlantic fortresses. *Lorraine*'s last combat was on 15 April 1945 when she bombarded the Point de Grave near the Royan Atlantic pocket, defended by German troops left behind in France the previous summer to deny the use of ports to the Allies.

American soldier standing in front of a 340mm coastal battery at Cap Cépet, which protected the seaward approaches to Toulon. During Operation *Dragoon*, *Lorraine* on several occasions targeted this battery, whose guns ironically the Germans had salvaged from *Lorraine*'s sistership *Provence*. (National Archives and Record Administration 80-G-364091)

The French battleship that saw the most extensive service alongside the Allies was the *Richelieu*. In February 1943 *Richelieu* arrived at the New York Naval Yard for comprehensive repairs and modernization. The 380mm guns damaged at Dakar in 1940 were replaced with ones removed from *Jean Bart*'s single operational turret. *Richelieu*'s aircraft facilities were removed as well as her French-made anti-aircraft guns, and these were replaced with 56 40mm Bofors guns mounted in 14 quadruple turrets and 48 single-mount 20mm Oerlikon anti-aircraft cannon. Once her refit was complete *Richelieu* was sent to reinforce the Royal Navy's Home Fleet at Scapa Flow in November 1943. The only sortie which *Richelieu* conducted while based in Scotland was escorting an unsuccessful carrier sweep against German shipping off the Norwegian coast from 10 to 12 February 1944 in an attempt to lure German surface units into combat. In March 1944 *Richelieu* was sent to Ceylon as part of a major reinforcement effort for the British Eastern Fleet where, ironically, she would come under the command of Admiral Somerville, who had commanded

Richelieu on trials off New York on 25 September 1943 following her extensive refit in the New York Navy Yard. (National Archives and Record Administration 19-LCM-84397)

the attacks on Mers el-Kébir in July 1940. Over the next several months *Richelieu* escorted three carrier raids against Sabang on Sumatra (Operation *Cockpit*, 16–21 April 1944), Soerabaya on Java (Operation *Transom*, 6–27 May 1944) and the Andaman Islands (Operation *Pedal*, 19–23 June 1944) and finally fired her guns against the Axis Powers for the first time during a naval bombardment of Sabang on 25 July (Operation *Crimson*). After sailing to French North Africa for a refit during the autumn of 1944, *Richelieu* returned to the Eastern Fleet for service in March 1945. Before the end of the war she participated in another bombardment of Sabang (Operation *Sunfish*, 9–20 April 1945), conducted bombardments against the Andaman and Nicobar Islands (Operation *Bishop*, 27 April–7 May 1945), and sailed against a sortie made by Japanese surface ships out of Singapore on 15–16 May (Operation *Dukedom*). *Richelieu* finally returned to France on 11 February 1946, the only battleship to have fought both the Allies and the Axis Powers during the war.

CONCLUSION

It goes without saying that the battleships of the Marine Nationale had very confused and unique experiences due to the confused and unique ordeal faced by the French in World War II. As a result, the battleships suffered a variety of fates. At Toulon, *Provence* was refloated and partially broken up; her hull was sunk by the Germans as a blockship in Toulon harbour in August 1944, but she was raised in 1949 and eventually scrapped. American aerial bombardments in 1944 damaged or sank the remaining battleships at Toulon. *Condorcert* and the dreadnought *Jean Bart*, renamed *Océan* in 1936 so that the name could pass on to the new battleship, served as training and accommodation vessels until they were fatally damaged in an air raid and were subsequently sunk on an even keel by the Germans on 15 March to prevent them from capsizing; both were refloated and broken up after the war. *Dunkerque* was partially scrapped during the summer of 1943 while still in the Vauban graving dock. Throughout the first half of 1944 she was heavily damaged by American bombing raids and by the end of the war was

Admiral James Somerville, commander of the British Eastern Fleet, boarding his flagship *Queen Elizabeth* off Ceylon. *Richelieu* is shown in the background. (© IWM A 23481)

little more than a battered hulk; what was left of her wreck was finally scrapped in 1958. *Strasbourg*, which had been refloated by an Italian salvage company in July 1943, was sunk by American bombers on 18 April 1944. *Strasbourg* was again refloated in the autumn of 1945, and after being used as a target for underwater explosive tests was finally broken up in 1955.

After serving as an anti-aircraft platform in Portsmouth during the Battle of Britain and the Blitz, *Courbet* was disarmed and turned over to the Royal Navy for use as a target vessel by the Fleet Air Arm. On 9 June 1944 *Courbet* was scuttled off Ouistreham along with other older vessels to create a breakwater for the Allies' Normandy beachhead. From a distance she did not appear to be sunk and, ironically, *Courbet* was the subject of several German attacks, including a Marder midget submarine attack on 17 August. The wreck was partially salvaged in the 1950s. *Paris* served as an accommodation vessel in Britain from July 1940 and was returned to the control of the Marine Nationale in July 1945, relocating to Brest a month later. She was used as a depot ship for the 2e Région Maritime until December 1955 and was broken up the following year. *Lorraine* remained in active service after World War II, serving as a gunnery training ship until July 1950 when she was redesignated as an accommodation vessel. She was decommissioned in late 1952 and scrapped the following year. *Jean Bart* returned to France in August 1945 and after four years of repair and reconstruction was finally formally commissioned on 16 January 1949. She primarily saw service as a gunnery training vessel, but she did participate in a limited role with the British and French naval forces off Egypt during the Suez Crisis in 1956. The ship was placed in reserve the following year, decommissioned in 1968 and scrapped in 1970. *Richelieu* served briefly off Indochina during the French post-war attempt to regain control of the colony, but primarily served as a training vessel. She was placed in reserve in 1958, decommissioned in 1968 and broken up that same year. With the exception of the United States Navy, the Marine Nationale kept its fast battleships in service longer than any other naval power.

BIBLIOGRAPHY

Auphan, Paul and Mordal, Jacques, *The French Navy in World War II*, United States Naval Institute, Annapolis (1959)

Bell, Christopher M. and Elleman, Bruce A. (eds), *Naval Mutinies of the Twentieth Century: An International Perspective*, Frank Cass, London (2003)

Bertke, Donald A., Kindell, Don and Smith, Gordon, *World War II Sea War. Volume 2: France Falls, Britain Stands Alone*, Bertke Publications, Dayton (2009)

Chesneau, Roger, *Conway's All the World's Fighting Ships 1922–1946*, Conway Maritime Press Ltd, London (1980)

Dumas, Robert and Guiglini, Jean, *Les cuirassés français des 23.500 tonnes*: Courbet – Jean Bart – Paris – France – Bretagne – Provence – Lorraine, Editions des 4 Seigneurs, Grenoble (1980)

Facon, Patrick, 'Le sursis de Mers el Kébir' in *Le Fana de l'Aviation* 11 (1999), pp.22–31

Friedman, Norman, *Naval Weapons of World War One: Guns, Torpedoes, Mines and ASW Weapons of All Nations, An Illustrated Directory*, Seaforth Publishing, Barnsley (2011)

Garzke, William H., Jr and Dulin, Robert O., Jr, *Battleships: Allied Battleships of World War II*, Naval Institute Press, Annapolis (1980)

Greene, Jack and Massignani, Alessandro, *The Naval War in the Mediterranean 1940–1943*, Chatham Publishing, London (1998)

Grey, Randal (ed.) et al, *Conway's All the World's Fighting Ships, 1906–1921*, Conway Maritime Press Ltd, London (1985)

Halpern, Paul G., *The Mediterranean Naval Situation 1908–1914*, Harvard University Press, Cambridge (1971)

Halpern, Paul G., *The Naval War in the Mediterranean, 1914–1918*, Naval Institute Press, Annapolis (1987)

Halpern, Paul G., *A Naval History of World War I*, United States Naval Institute, Annapolis (1994)

Jordan, John and Caresse, Philippe, *French Battleships of World War One*, Naval Institute Press, Annapolis (2017)

Jordan, John and Dumas, Robert, *French Battleships: 1922–1956*, Seaforth Publishing, Barnsley (2014)

Lasterle, Philippe, 'Could Admiral Gensoul Have Averted the Tragedy of Mers el-Kébir?' in *The Journal of Military History* 67, no. 3 (2003), pp.835–44

Le Comte, J., 'L'affaire de la *Zenta*' in *Revue maritime* 204 (1963), pp.1254–59

Marder, Arthur J., *Operation Menace. The Dakar Expedition and the Dudley North Affair*, Oxford University Press, London (1976)

Marder, Arthur J., *From the Dardanelles to Oran: Studies of the Royal Navy in War and Peace, 1915–1940*, Seaforth Publishing, Barnsley (2015)

Masson, Philippe, *La marine française et la mer noire (1918–1919)*, Publications de la Sorbonne, Paris (1982)

Millett, Allan R. and Murray, Williamson (eds), *Military Effectiveness. Volume II: The Interwar Period*, Allan & Unwin, Boston (1988)

Morison, Samuel Eliot, *History of United States Naval Operations in World War II, Volume Two: Operations in North African Waters October 1942–June 1943*, Little, Brown and Company, Boston (1951)

Newbolt, Henry, *History of the Great War: Naval Operations Volume IV*, Longmans, Green and Co., London (1928)

O'Hara, Vincent P., 'The Battle of Casablanca: The Marine Nationale versus the US Navy' in Jordan, John (ed.), *Warship 2011*, Conway, London (2011), pp.48–63

Robb-Webb, Jon, *The British Pacific Fleet: Experience and Legacy, 1944–1950*, Ashgate, Farnham (2013)

Roksund, Arne, *The Jeune École: The Strategy of the Weak*, Brill, Leiden (2007)

Ropp, Theodore, *The Development of a Modern Navy: French Navy Policy 1871–1904*, Naval Institute Press, Annapolis (1987)

Salaun, Vice-Amiral Henri, *La marine française*, Les Éditions de France, Paris (1934)

Toussaint, Patrick, 'Mers el-Kébir: La Royale Navy attaque la flotte française!' in *LOS! Le magazine de la guerre navale, aéronavale, et sous-marine* 35 (2017), pp.24–41

Willmott, H. P., *The Last Century of Sea Power, Volume 2: From Washington to Tokyo, 1922–1945*, Indiana University Press, Bloomington (2010)

INDEX

Note: locators in bold refer to plates,
illustrations and captions.